THE JET LAG BOOK

Also by Don Kowet

The Black Badge: Confessions of a Case Worker, 1969
Golden Toes: Football's Greatest Kickers, 1972
Vida Blue, 1974
Pele, 1975
The Soccer Book, 1976
The Rich Who Own Sports, 1977
Franco Harris: A Biography, 1977
The Seventh Game, 1978
How to Watch Soccer, 1979

THE JET LAG BOOK

Don Kowet

Crown Publishers, Inc.
New York

Published by Crown Publishers, Inc., One Park Avenue, New York, New York 10016 and simultaneously in Canada by General Publishing Company Limited

Manufactured in the United States of America

Library of Congress Cataloging in Publication Data

Kowet, Don.
    The jet lag book.

    Includes index.
    1. Jet lag. I. Title.
RC1076.J48K68 1983   613.6'8   83-1805
ISBN 0-517-54895-X

Design by Leonard Henderson

10 9 8 7 6 5 4 3 2 1

First Edition

ACKNOWLEDGMENTS

Grateful acknowledgment is hereby given to the following individuals and publishers for the use of excerpted materials quoted in this book: David Frost ● Harry Reasoner ● Jim McKay ● Don Ohlmeyer ● "How to Feast and Fast in Flight" by Barbara Dubivsky, © 1982 by The New York Times Company. Reprinted by permission of The New York Times Company. ● "On the Move: Jet Lag," *People Weekly*, June 28, 1982, copyright © 1982 by Time, Inc. Reprinted by permission of Time, Inc. ● "Exercise in the Chair" reprinted by permission of Scandinavian Airlines. ● "Jet Lag: The New Solutions" by Marylou Bondon Dodge, copyright © 1979 The Hearst Corporation. Courtesy of *Harper's Bazaar*. ● "Cleaning the Ear" by Dr. Karl Neumann reprinted by permission of TRAVEL/HOLIDAY, Travel Building, Floral Park, New York, and by Dr. Karl Neumann. ● "Fitness in the Chair" reprinted by permission of Lufthansa German Airlines. ● "How Time-zone Changes Can Shake Up Travellers' Health" by Dr. David Moreau, copyright © 1971 by the Condé Nast Publications, Inc. Reprinted by permission of the author. ● "My Home Time Zone Blues" by Doug Wilson. Reprinted by permission of the author. ● "Is There Life after 40 for Pro Athletes?" by Don Kowet, copyright © 1982 by Triangle Publications, Inc. Courtesy of *TV Guide*. ● "Jet Lag Isn't Just a State of Mind" by Roy Rowan, *Fortune*, August 1976, copyright © 1976 by Time, Inc. ● "Shuttle Fatigue," *Time*, April 26, 1982, copyright © 1982 by Time, Inc. Reprinted by permission of Dr. W. Gerald Auten. ● "What It Takes to Be a Top Fashion Model" by Christie Brinkley, copyright © 1982 by Triangle Publications, Inc. Courtesy of *TV Guide*. ● "Coach John Madden's New Calling" by Steve Gelman, copyright © 1983 by Triangle Publications, Inc. Courtesy of *TV Guide*. ● "What Hath Night to Do with Sleep" by Martin C. Moore-Ede, reprinted by permission of *Natural History*, Vol. 91, No. 9, copyright © 1982 American Museum of Natural History.

To my friend Shashi, a modern Marco Polo.

Contents

THE JET LAG BOOK

Introduction

I was sitting in an airplane beside a powerful executive of one of our three television networks. We were discussing why so much of our prime-time programming seems so silly or simple-minded. Every fall, the networks issue déjà vu schedules cluttered with copycat sitcoms and mindless made-for-TV movies and squadrons of hero cops, only slightly more civilized and convincing than the killer cartoon-characters we let babysit each Saturday morning.

How, I wondered, could so many intellectually curious men and women—TV executives with seasonal opera subscriptions on both coasts; beneficiaries of the wisdom imparted at prestigious universities; able to doll up their dialogue with (admittedly, well-rehearsed) sayings from, say, Disraeli or Shakespeare—how could they so cynically serve us so much . . . well . . . plain garbage?

In explanation, the executive coolly opened his mental "media bag" and withdrew the appropriate clichés: an advertiser-supported medium needs more than a medium-size audience for every program; each viewer retains the inalienable right to lift his rump off that roost in his TV room and either cast a negative Nielsen ballot by switching to another channel or—God forbid!—deliver a vote of total "no confidence" by turning the damn TV set off.

Then the words ebbed. The executive leaned back in his seat— a hundred dollars' costlier, because a half-an-inch wider, than the foam-fortified cradles crushing the folks behind us in economy class. He paused, the space where his speech had been now bursting with the roar of airplane engines, flinging us, at thirty-five thousand feet, through the stratosphere from one coast toward the other.

"You want to know why we *really* make so many lousy programming decisions?" he said. The corners of his mouth curved in a sly grin. "Because of this," he added, his outstretched arm slicing an arc that encompassed his fellow first-class passengers (I was only a temporary visitor, tolerated because the seat next to my companion was empty) cowering in their chairs, the flight attendants dispensing free potions of alcoholic amnesia. "We're all suffering from jet lag."

The executive was joking, of course. Still, in the humor there was the hint of a truth. Television executives shuttle from Los Angeles to New York, and from nation to nation, as casually as the rest of us commute from suburbs to the sweat shops where we earn our wages.

During what was left of our flight to New York, the executive delivered to me a wry litany of the symptoms he suffered: the occasional memory lapses, the dumb business deals, the embarrassment of being caught snoring in the middle of a crucial conference after jetting across fifteen time zones from New York to Sydney, Australia—all side effects, he assured me, of jet lag. He had been kidding about jet lag's impact on programming; he was dead serious about its impact on programmers.

"You know," he told me, as the NO SMOKING sign lighted up and we began our descent, "they say you can reduce the effect of jet lag by going on Concorde. With the supersonic, I can fly across the Atlantic, do a day's work, and be home by bedtime. The problem is," he added, "I've read that scientists say speeding along at an altitude of between fifty- and sixty-thousand feet, the human body can withstand only sixty-one transatlantic round trips a year. It isn't the jet lag; its the galactic radiation. How much," he said, "is supersonic flight going to shorten my life span?"

I'll admit it: at the time, I had trouble mustering more than a cosmetic sympathy. The man was earning about a million dollars a year. And, as far as life spans go, when you're earning that kind of money, I think you can probably make up in quality what you lose in quantity. The little sympathy I did feel evaporated at the curb outside Kennedy Airport. The executive climbed into his chauffeur-driven limousine. I hailed the only taxi cab in sight. Like so many of his New York City brethren, the cabbie didn't speak much English. Judging by the name on his hack license, he was of Slavic descent and probably a recent immigrant. Why else, after I had clearly told him I wanted to go westbound to Manhattan, did he insist on taking eastbound turns that, except for the Atlantic Ocean, would have brought us to beautiful downtown Budapest?

That night, my wife and I shared a good laugh at the TV executive's suggestion—only half tongue-in-cheek—that the junk on television was, in part, attributable to jet lag. Then, a week later, after I had undertaken a series of short but tiring business flights, my wife and I flew off on vacation. The flight was a chartered one. That meant the seating arrangement in our Douglas DC-9 was six across—three-and-three, each trio separated by the aisle. Unfortunately, the aisle wasn't wide enough to prevent the cute kid in the aisle seat across from my wife's from reaching over and yanking a tuft of her hair every time she turned to talk to me. It didn't matter, though. I couldn't answer her anyway, without waking up the man in the window seat who kept falling asleep on my shoulder.

When the cabin lights dimmed for the movie, the man next to me awoke, turned on his light, and began skimming through a newspaper. The seats were so narrow I had to read the *Boston Globe*, too. My wife's attempt to watch the movie ended when the cute kid across from her ripped off her earphones (for the third time) and bounded joyfully away, down the aisle toward the front of the plane. The child's mother, understandably, made no effort to retrieve him. My wife, herself a mother, understood. She did not try to recover either the child or her earphones. Besides, there was so much smoke in the air, the figures on the screen were ghostly and flickering. It was like trying to watch your television when the master antenna is unplugged. We passed the time by eating anything and everything the harried flight attendants placed on our trays. We had wine with our meal, and, for dessert, I downed a couple of daiquiris.

We had left New York at 10 P.M.; we arrived in London, after a six-hour flight, at 10 A.M., my wife sleepy, while I was too hung over to be sleepy. I had only imbibed two watered-down cocktails and a thimbleful of wine, yet my head felt as if there were a Lilliputian Harlem Globetrotter, giving the crowd his dribble-between-the-legs routine, right behind my temples. An hour later we stumbled out of customs and into our rented car. In spite of the fact that I would periodically spot oncoming automobiles heading straight toward the center of my radiator grille and would realize I had drifted onto the "wrong" side of the road, our journey toward Manchester, where we were going to visit friends, went smoothly for a while. Until, that is, I encountered my first "round-about."

A round-about is what the English call a traffic circle. Although I had once lived in London for three years, suddenly I could not remember whether I was supposed to hug the round-about's circumference by circling it from the left or from the right. I solved that problem, much to the surprise of English drivers putting toward me, by directing my car straight over the round-about, hitting my head against the roof as we bumped along, but miraculously avoiding any head-on collisions.

Finally, we reached the sanctuary of our friends' home in Manchester. There we relaxed, for about a half hour, until my wife and I, indignant over some imagined slight, sparked a silly argument that left our friends stunned—and ourselves huffily departing, to lodge that night at a hotel.

The next morning, after a full night's sleep, though a fitful one, I telephoned my friend to apologize for having put on what the English call "a bad show." My friend, himself a world traveler, said, "It was jet lag."

Intrigued by the phenomenon, and convinced, I began discussing it with the inveterate air travelers I met in the course of writing articles for *TV Guide*. Actors, executives, newsmen, advertising creative directors, fashion designers, professional athletes—many of them, I soon learned, were as preoccupied with the subject as the TV executive who had first piqued my interest. Almost all of them were obsessed with jet lag's sensations and symptoms and physiological side effects.

Jim McKay, host of ABC's "Wide World of Sports," who logs at least two hundred fifty thousand air miles every year, told me about the sometimes hilarious, other times nightmarish, perils of performing before the TV cameras when your mind is trailing a continent behind your body. Christie Brinkley, the star model, revealed to me some of the stratagems she's devised to keep from looking like Bela Lugosi after being cooped up in an airplane cabin for seven hours or more. From the scientists studying this syndrome—NASA alone has conducted more than four thousand jet lag–related studies; orbiting astronauts suffer the same symptoms that bedevil us lower-altitude Lindberghs—I learned ways to placate this invisible, unwelcome airborne companion. Perhaps even more important than the right answers, I learned some of the right questions to ask—to ask myself and to ask you.

Do long jet flights to the east or to the west leave you feeling irritable? Do you find yourself falling asleep on a museum tour and being wide awake at midnight? Does your memory often lapse during a business lunch abroad? Do math problems an eighth-grader could solve suddenly seem as knotty as any unraveled by Einstein? And how about your inner body rhythms— do hunger, thirst, elimination, and sex drive start marching to a different drummer?

Scientific surveys show that if you answered yes to all of these questions, you are in agreement with most transcontinental travelers. If you answered no, scientific experiments prove, you are simply fooling yourself. No matter how macho an airborne Marco Polo, no matter how physically fit or how frequent a flier, you cannot escape that implacable malady called jet lag.

"There is *no* permanent physiological adaptation to jet lag," said Dr. Timothy Crawford, a former navy flight surgeon and crew physician to United Airlines. "There is only a *mental* adjustment to the routine."

Frequent travelers may get used to feeling irritable and incompetent and exhausted, but the mere fact of frequent travel can't slay jet lag's symptoms. *No one is immune*, not even the pilot controlling your airplane—and your fate.

Exactly how endangered by jet lag are you? The answer depends on what specific species of airborne traveler you belong to. To find out, answer the questions in the Jet Lag Vulnerability Profile that follows in chapter 1.

I

Before You Board

Jet Lag Vulnerability Profile

Instructions: On the list below, circle the number of every state-ment or question that applies to you. (In some sections there may be more than one question or statement that describes you; circle as many as apply.)

Age
You are
1. Under 30
2. Between 30 and 40
3. Between 40 and 60
4. Over 60

Rhythms
You are
5. A night owl
6. An early bird
7. Rigid in your eating and sleeping habits

Preflight Preparedness
Will you
8. Complete your packing, ticket purchases, reservations—all the preflight routine—at least two days in advance of departure?
9. Be doing many things at the last minute?
10. Get to the airport with at least an hour to spare before flight time?
11. Have to rush to catch your plane?
12. Carry with you a special medical kit to counter the worst side effects of jet travel?
13. Begin, days before your departure, a special diet to help reset your inner clocks?

Destination
You
14. Will be traveling eastward
15. Will be traveling westward
16. Will be traveling for business

During the Flight
EATING
You plan to
17. Eat only the food you bring on board
18. Eat no food at all till you arrive at your destination
19. Eat as sparingly as possible
20. Eat the full airline meals served on the plane
21. Chew gum

DRINKING
You usually
22. Don't drink any beverage at all
23. Drink coffee or tea
24. Drink soft drinks
25. Drink only water or fruit juices
26. Drink wine or liquor

SMOKING
You are
27. A nonsmoker
28. A smoker

COMPANIONSHIP
You will be
29. Embarking alone on a group tour
30. Traveling alone
31. Traveling with someone of the opposite sex
32. Traveling with a business companion of the same sex

SOCIABILITY
You
33. Often strike up conversations with strangers on the plane
34. Usually keep to yourself throughout the flight

R & R

You generally

35. Stay in your seat during most of the flight
36. Get up and move around a lot
37. Perform sets of in-seat exercises
38. Try to sleep or nap from time to time
39. Rent the airline earphones and watch the movie, or listen to in-flight music and talk channels
40. Catch up on your business or school paperwork

SEATING LOCATION

You will

41. Be traveling first class
42. Be traveling coach class
43. Be choosing your seat on board with the aid of an airline seating plan

At the Destination

On the day you arrive, you will probably

44. Begin seeing the sights
45. Have to make important business decisions
46. Rent a car
47. Stop over at least one night before continuing your journey
48. Catch another flight
49. Eat food that you are not accustomed to eating
50. Engage in sexual intercourse

Key: To find your score, add together the points listed below beside the number for each question you circled on the Vulnerability Profile.

Add

1. 15
2. 20
3. 30
4. 35
5. Westward flight: minus 5; Eastward flight: 0
6. Eastward flight: minus 5; Westward flight: 0
7. 10
8. 5

9. 15
10. 5
11. 15
12. 0
13. Minus 15
14. 30
15. 15
16. 15
17. 5
18. 15
19. 10
20. 20
21. 5
22. 25
23. 10
24. 10
25. 0
26. Westbound: add 10; Eastbound: add 20. Add 10 more for each additional drink.
27. 5
28. 20
29. 10
30. 15
31. 0
32. 5
33. 5
34. 15
35. 25
36. 5
37. Minus 15
38. 0
39. 15
40. 20
41. Minus 5
42. 10
43. 0
44. 10
45. 25
46. 20
47. 0

48. 10
49. 15
50. Minus 5

Your Jet Lag Vulnerability Score

50 or under	Excellent	Smooth Flying Ahead
51–100	Good	Expect Only Minor Body-clock Turbulence
101–200	Fair	Belt up for Some Rough Weather
201–300	Poor	You're Heading for a Nosedive
301-and-above	Awful	Unless you get smart and change your airborne ways, *You're Gonna Be a Basket-Case*

2

Jet Lag in History

If you proved, in our test, to be vulnerable to the pitfalls of long-distance travel, console yourself with the knowledge that you are in good company. One of the grievances cited by the signers of the Declaration of Independence against King George III of England was that "he has called together legislative bodies at places unusual, uncomfortable and distant from the depository of their public records, for the sole purpose of fatiguing them into compliance with his measures." Since the dawn of this republic, citizens have been complaining about one form or another of travel fatigue.

Of course, the founding fathers didn't have machines that could go far enough, fast enough to encounter the phenomenon we now call jet lag. Yet even before the advent of the jet engine (and its transformation, after World War II, of commercial aviation), early travelers were noting something strange and inexplicable. In 1931, during his around-the-world flight, Wiley Post realized that whenever he landed his monoplane, *Winnie Mae*, he was out of sync with the natives. His hosts would be setting the table (or reed mat) for supper; Post's body would be telling him it was time to sleep.

Soon it wasn't just pilots and their passengers who were experiencing this sensation of being out of step with the external environment. On the ground, Edison's invention of the light bulb had liberated men from the fumes and eyestrains caused by gas lamps and candles. But, as so often happens with any beneficial advance in technology, there was a price to pay.

Able now to light up their factories throughout the night, industrialists realized that it was often cheaper to keep their production lines humming in nonstop twenty-four-hour cycles. It might take several days to fire a blast furnace, so it made sense to keep the furnace glowing continually once it was heated up. Thus, thanks to Thomas Edison, workers began toiling in ever-rotating shifts. Like Wiley Post, shift workers soon discovered that their internal cadences—their rhythms of hunger and wakefulness—were marching to a different drummer.

During World War II, the need for more and more guns and ammunition at the front intensified the trend to round-the-clock work. By the end of the war, we were living in a society that increasingly ignored the day-night cycle of the natural world around us. The factory lights didn't dim; in the sky above us, jet airplanes were hurtling us across multiple time zones, unexpectedly plunging our bodies into night when they expected daylight. Wiley Post had reduced Phineas Fogg's fictional eighty-day around-the-world record to slightly more than a week. Thirty-four years after Post's world-girdling flight aboard the *Winnie Mae*, astronauts Virgil Grissom and John Young were orbiting the earth, in *Gemini III*, once every eighty-eight minutes.

Man had built supersonic airplanes able to shatter the sound barrier. But the biological speed barrier inside his own body remained impenetrable. Whenever he exceeded the velocity of approximately four hundred miles per hour, traveling east or west, odd biological and behavioral symptoms began surfacing. Businessmen displayed them. So did opera stars, oil engineers, advertising executives, rock musicians—any professional often on the wing might become stricken. And, ironically, none suffered more than those historic veterans of travel fatigue: diplomats and politicians.

Beginning in the 1950s, the men whose profession is government started shuttling between remote outposts, their gypsy journeys more perverse a torture than any mere mean king could conjure up. One of shuttle diplomacy's earliest practitioners was Secretary of State John Foster Dulles. After a grueling series of intercontinental hops, in 1956, Dulles landed in Washington in time to learn that Egypt—his main port-of-call those past months—had just agreed to buy a substantial quantity of armaments from the USSR. Dulles immediately sent for the Egyptian ambassador. On the spot, Dulles canceled the agreement he had made with Egypt's Nasser, pledging that the United States would bankroll Egypt's ambitious Aswan project, damming up the Nile.

Dulles's decision catalyzed a historic chain reaction. The Egyptians, enraged, nationalized the Suez Canal. Britain, France, and Israel responded by sending in troops to recapture from Egypt the crucial waterway. The crisis gripped world attention.

Years later, in an interview with columnist Marquis Childs, Dulles admitted that he had made a mistake. He had acted too hastily, he said ... because he was suffering from a severe case of jet lag. More recently, because of jet lag, Hawaii Senator Hiram Fong retired after seventeen years on Capitol Hill. The senator, who made the ninety-seven-hundred-mile trip to Washington and back nine times a year, told a reporter it took him nearly a week to recover from each leg of the journey—eighteen weeks a year "in purgatory, trying to get back to normal."

Jet lag: the malaise of modern air travelers, as scurvy was of ancient seafaring ones. Everyone who flies east or west several hours or more by jet suffers from this nagging physical disease. Few know how to cope with it. Few even know they are suffering from this malady, or what causes it.

WHAT CAUSES JET LAG?

Jet lag, or "circadian dysrhythmia," may be a recent phenomenon, but its roots are as ancient as the universe itself. (*Circadian* comes from the Latin word *circa,* meaning "approximately," and *dies,* meaning "day"; *dysrhythmia* means "out of sync.") The universe is in constant cyclical motion; the galaxy our sun belongs to takes about two hundred million years to return to the same place in space. Within each galaxy, billions of suns revolve around a center; within each solar system, planets circle their suns. And so it goes, right down to the atom, in which electrons are orbiting a nucleus at tremendous speeds.

Jet lag's roots lie in this cyclical nature of the universe, as well as in the special conditions of our own evolution.

Dr. Martin C. Moore-Ede, professor in the Department of Physiology and Biophysics of the Harvard Medical School, wrote in *Nature* magazine: "We carry within us models of the earth's rotation and the day-night cycle under which our species evolved."

From our molecular structure on upward, our bodies are composed of thousands of systems, each with its own cyclical rhythm. Temperature, heart rate, perspiration, blood and urine composition, digestion, elimination, metabolism—each system has its own inherent tidelike ebb and flow, peaking sometime during the day, slowing down at night, in approximate twenty-four-hour cycles that correspond to the earth's rotation around the sun. For their smooth functioning, these internal systems of ours depend on external cues of light and darkness.

Our brains contain pacemakers charged with ensuring that a system's ebb and flow stays in sync with the day-night cycle. For instance, a pair of these pacemakers regulate our sleep cycle. Scientists believe that one sleep regulator is in the hypothalamus, within two tiny clusters of ten thousand nerve cells each (the suprachiasmatic nuclei), located where the optic nerves intersect en route from our eyes to the visual cortices of our brain. Unless acted upon by some external time cue, this internal clock completes a full cycle about every twenty-five hours. "However, under normal conditions, it is reset by about an hour each day by the light-dark cycle, via a specialized bundle of nerves (the retino-hypothalamic tract) passing back from the eyes," said Dr. Moore-Ede in *Nature.*

This pacemaker helps determine the time you start to feel sleepy, and it helps ensure that once you fall asleep, you'll remain so until morning comes. Without this timekeeper, your sleep might be broken into many episodes, instead of a single uninterrupted one.

The other internal timekeeper regulating our sleep patterns scientists simply call "X," since, although they have proved this pacemaker's existence, they have been unable to pinpoint its exact location. X's task is to regulate arousal from sleep; it helps determine how long you slumber. X takes its cue from the circadian rhythm of our body temperature, which wanes in the early morning hours, then begins to warm up our bodies until we wake up, finally peaking sometime in the late afternoon. At the appropriate point in this temperature rise, the X "alarm clock" triggers our arousal from sleep.

Under normal conditions, these pacemakers stick to their own time cycles, no matter how much you shake and jar them. If you party all night, then flop down hoping for eight hours of sleep early the next morning, these internal timekeepers will give you an unwelcome call within an hour or so of your usual wake-up time. Yet all you have to do to gum up their works is climb aboard a jet plane bound, east or west, for some distant locale. By the time you land, these implacable internal pacemakers will be about as trustworthy timekeepers as your kitchen clock after your three-year-old son has "cleaned" its innards with olive oil. Thrust into a foreign light-dark cycle, all your internal timekeepers—the regulators not just of sleep and wakefulness but every other biological function—suddenly start receiving faulty external cues, setting off an enormous chemical disturbance in your body. Your billions of internal clocks are receiving signals to which they respond collectively in a confused fashion, causing bodily distress.

NO JET LAG NORTH AND SOUTH

"If God had intended man to fly around the earth," a pilot once remarked, "He would have made the equator run north and south."

Flights due north or south do not in any way affect your internal time clocks, since your airplane does not transgress any new time zones. Birds, unlike humans, instinctively avoid severe "desynchronosis" in flight by traveling mostly north and south in their migrations. When the swallows return to Capistrano, or the golden plovers of Canada migrate to Brazil, they limit their movement east or west to a maximum of four time zones. The Norwegian snow goose that flies from Norway to Labrador and back avoids disrupting its internal rhythms because its entire route remains within the twilight zone of the Arctic.

Senior airplane pilots, it seems, are probably just as smart as birds. They have first choice of flight routes over their more junior colleagues and, studies show, prefer to fly north-south routes in order to avoid the complications that east-west travel inflicts on their body clocks.

WEST IS BEST

Of the two airborne directional evils transcontinental travelers face, flying westward is the lesser one. Jetting from New York to California, you see the sun seeming to rise at a later hour, which means your internal pacemakers are merely receiving their reset signals a little later than usual. Your day has simply become three hours longer. Although you will feel the effects of jet lag, the symptoms will be far less acute than after an eastbound trip.

Why Is West Best?

Scientists offer two reasons why westbound travel may be easier on your body than eastbound travel. First, experiments with volunteers immersed in environments void of any time cues have proved that our natural rhythms tend to run slightly longer than twenty-four hours. Thus, it stands to reason that our bodies will adapt more easily to a longer day on a westbound flight than a shorter one heading east. Second, and perhaps more crucial, westbound passengers tend to arrive at their destinations (at least those travelers flying from our East to West Coasts) in time to go to sleep when the natives do. If you leave New York in the morning, say, you arrive in San Francisco early in the afternoon. You slept the night before. Now all you have to do is go through the day and sleep when the natives sleep. At worst, your body should be awake only three hours after the natives are counting sheep. Obviously, it's an advantage to leave on a trip soon after you've had a full night's sleep.

EAST IS WORST

Going eastward, however, most travelers tend to depart in the evening after work. You arrive at your destination the next morning, bleary-eyed and bloated, without having been able to enjoy a real night's sleep. You have to stumble through your first day abroad, fighting to keep your eyelids propped open.

Furthermore, traveling east, your internal body clocks suffer massive trauma. Eastbound, the sun seems to rise earlier (rather than later, as in westbound journeys), which means your brain is being asked to start a brand-new day six or seven hours or more earlier than its pacemakers are accustomed to. You are awake and eating on the plane, but your body temperature, hormone flow, and other vital functions are still clinging stubbornly to home time. Your night has been sliced in half; your new "day" is going to be an interminable one.

CABIN CONDITIONS AND JET LAG

Westbound or eastbound, your suffering doesn't start in the air. Only when your body lands and discovers the unnatural relationship between its own internal time and external, geographic time, does the pain begin. But conditions in the airplane can make that pain much worse. The airplane cabin's heat and low (sometimes zero) humidity dehydrate your body. Your respiratory passages and ocular fluids dry out, resulting in scratchy throats and dimming vision. In extreme cases, especially when you smoke tobacco and imbibe alcoholic beverages during the flight, cabin conditions can cause your nails and hair to turn brittle, and induce "hypoxia" (oxygen deficiency, leading to a lessening of mental ability and accuracy), mild amnesia (at least for recent events), and temporary anemia.

Once on the ground, at your destination, you need to be in peak physical and mental condition to weather the welcoming gauntlet of baggage retrieval, customs, taxi lines, city traffic, and hotel check-in. But your body's inner rhythms are out of step with the environment. You have crossed too many time zones too quickly. (Each new time zone adds an hour to your day going west and subtracts one from your day going east.) Over the next five to fourteen days (depending on whether your trip was westbound or eastbound), you are liable to make a business deal that you'll live to regret; tests show that soundness of judgment, for sufferers of jet lag, may be 20 percent lower than that of your best performance. Or maybe you won't live to regret that dumb deal, after all. Routine activities, such as driving a car, suddenly turn risky; tests prove that manual dexterity is even more seriously impaired than judgment.

You may be lethargic. You can't get to sleep, and when you do start dozing, you wake up far sooner than you had intended. You're ready for lunch when the natives are nibbling at their croissants and sipping bitter Turkish coffee. When they are gorging themselves on a saucy dinner, you are trying like hell to keep awake; battling to keep your head from falling into your soup. Your sex life has become a tangle it would take Masters and Johnson to unravel, and your relationship with your partner of the opposite gender is not improved when, after ten years, you suddenly forget his/her first name. That day trip you planned to Versailles will just have to be postponed while you scour Paris in search of a bottle of Pepto-Bismol.

But at your worst moments, remember: you are now experiencing what the movers and shakers of this planet—the celebrity athletes, politicians, all those jet-setters—endure every time they embark on one of their glamorous grand tours.

Fat chance! The rich *are* different from you and me, and not only because they have more money. The jet-setters, obsessed with the ill effects of modern air travel, have devised tactics to thwart it. In the chapters that follow, you'll get their tips on how to cope with jet lag when you contract the disease, and advice from doctors and scientists on how to avoid being ravaged by this plague in the first place.

3

Picking Your Flight

It is the dawn of your long-awaited departure by air for two weeks in Paris. You have made every conceivable effort to ensure that your vacation—costing as much as three or four thousand dollars for a couple—will be a satisfactory one. You have purchased your airline tickets or booked your tour. You have the confirmation slip proving you are entitled to a reserved room—in a Left Bank hotel or a more luxurious one. Your new set of matching luggage sits yawning on your bedroom floor, like a school of famished fish waiting to be fed. Unfortunately, though, you are yawning, too. Last-minute preparations kept you hopping half the night. Last-minute details and your dread of flying: being encapsulated in a silver cylinder, hurtling through the thin air for six or more hours. In the medicine cabinet, alongside the toothpaste and other toiletries you plan to pack, is a bottle of tranquilizers.

You have thought of everything—except jet lag. You have forgotten that with every time zone, your body will grow more and more out of sync with its surroundings. You will remember the malady when you reach your destination, wide awake at midnight, your stomach clamoring for lunch when everyone else is eating dinner. You will be feeling drowsy when the natives are painting the town. And those tempting morsels you'll wolf down during the flight, the movies and the music on board the aircraft, will only make the suffering worse when you land.

You should have begun combating jet lag days ago. The precautions you do—or don't—take in the days before your departure can determine whether your vacation or business trip turns out to be a bonanza or a bust.

CHOOSING YOUR FLIGHT

Whenever people ask me, I tell them the honest-to-Shakespeare truth: like many of my professional peers, I decided to become a writer when I realized that there was nothing else in life I could really do. Among my pitstops along the back road to career enlightenment were mercifully brief stints as a department-store floor manager (I was soon demoted to caretaker of the imported-cookie counter), welfare caseworker (so generously did I dispense your money, I may have personally brought New York City to the verge of bankruptcy), and temporary salesman for a soft-drink company (not exactly an apostle of the power-of-positive-thinking, I would tiptoe into a bar and say, "You don't need any Canada Dry, do you?"). But there was one job I enjoyed immensely. If the profession had paid more than a pittance, I would still be an airline reservations agent today.

Every caller offered a new set of complex routing problems I had to solve. If callers were pleasant and positive in their approach, I would spend all the time it took to thumb through my Official Airlines Guide and punch up my computer, till I came up with a series of connections that were dazzling in their logic and purity. Of course, once in a while a caller would be surly. We had ways of dealing with that. Say the caller demanded a "direct" flight between New York and San Francisco. I would give him a direct flight, all right—with thirteen stops, via Nome, Alaska. "Direct" is not the same as "nonstop."

Working the night shift, we would often get calls from drunks. If the inebriate gave us too hard a time, we would tell him: "Sir, why don't you drop dead. We'll ship you air freight."

Nevertheless, most passengers were friendly and forthright. Most reservations agents attempted to satisfy the passengers' needs. Unless you were trying to book a tour to a locale our airplanes didn't service, we could reserve a hotel room for you, rent a car, confirm your plane reservations—or tell you about flights on other airlines if ours didn't suit you. Too often, though, our flights did suit the caller. I say "too often," because airlines schedule the bulk of their flights to coincide with the peak flow of passenger traffic, not to coincide with the peaks and troughs of your internal body clocks.

For instance, most flights to Europe leave in the evening, so that travelers don't have to lose a day of work on the day of their departure. Unfortunately, that night flight is going to make your jet lag worse when you land. You lose a night's sleep, arrive at your destination in the morning, and have to endure an entire day (if you can stay awake) till the natives slip beneath their quilts.

So: If possible, pick a flight that arrives at your destination at the time closest to your regular bedtime.

Traveling eastbound, said "60 Minutes" correspondent Harry Reasoner, "You try to work your flight so that you have a long day instead of a short one. If you're going to London, for instance, it's a lot better to leave in the morning and get there in the late evening, rather than leaving at night, and getting there in the morning. And stay up," CBS's Reasoner added, "and go to bed at your normal time, so that you don't get yourself confused as to how many days have taken place."

The primary reason that experienced travelers are beginning to choose day flights over night flights when journeying to Europe is that sleep is such a marvelous healer. Departing during the day, you won't feel you've lost a night's sleep. Since the flight itself will be tiring—customs, taxis, hotel check-in, etc.—you may be exhausted enough to simply tumble into bed when you arrive and sleep while the natives are slumbering. When you awaken the next morning, your biological rhythms may be out of sync with everyone else's, but at least you'll start off the day in step with the rhythm of the city.

Traveling westbound, say from New York to San Francisco, your options are more flexible. You can time your arrival for late afternoon, West Coast time, weathering the stretched-out day to go to bed at the time the natives do. Or else, after a solid night's sleep, you can save a day of work and follow the strategy devised by Aer Lingus. In his column, in 1973, *Esquire's* then travel editor Richard Joseph assessed the Irish Airline's tactic for businessmen on brief working trips.

"I have enjoyed some success with the Irish Airlines system on short working trips to the West Coast from my base in New York," said Joseph. "Taking a flight around nine in the morning, I'll land in San Francisco, let's say, shortly after noon, Pacific time, and by the time I've checked into my room it's generally too late for a business lunch. Which is fine, because I will have had a morning snack and lunch on the plane. I try to set up an early dinner and to get to bed by 11 P.M.—which is 2 A.M. Eastern stomach time.

"If I'm planning to return east within a day or so," Joseph added, "I'll get up at five in the morning—eight o'clock in New York—and work or read for the couple of hours before local people start functioning, lunch promptly at noon, and get to bed early again, staying as close as possible to my eastern schedule. If not, I'll try to sleep late, lunch and dine late, go out on the town, and so absorb the three-hour time difference comfortably within a two-day span."

Other business travelers, flying from the West Coast to the East Coast, prefer to ship their bodies by the passenger equivalent of Federal Express overnight airmail—the "red eye" flights that regularly take off from, say, Los Angeles, sometime after 10 P.M., depositing the passenger in an East Coast city in the vicinity of 7 or 8 A.M. the following morning.

There are undeniable benefits from choosing a red-eye flight. However, they are outweighed by the liabilities.

Pluses

1. Workaholics don't have to suffer anxiety attacks worrying how the world of commerce is going to survive without them while they are imprisoned in an airplane for an entire afternoon. Traveling at night, they save the world from being deprived of their talents for even half a working day.

2. Skinflints can savor throughout the flight (if the East Coast is not their home base) the money they are saving by sleeping in the airplane, rather than in a costly hotel room.

3. Some "red eyes" offer their passengers free drinks, permitting a traveler to pass the boring six hours in the air by boozing himself into oblivion.

4. Often the airplane is comparatively empty. A passenger can raise the arms of the seats around him and flop down to sleep across three or four chairs.

Minuses

However, these benefits are, in my opinion, outweighed by a red eye's drawbacks:

1. If the East Coast is not your home base, and you need to check in to a hotel when you arrive, you are liable to spend considerable time sitting in the lobby. Unless your room was vacant the night before, it probably won't be ready for occupancy until after 11 A.M.

2. While sometimes a red eye is fairly empty, at other unpredictable times it may be so crowded that even a sardine (if it had elbows) wouldn't have elbowroom. In that case, only travelers who have spent nights practicing sleeping bolt-upright in chairs will be likely to arrive refreshed.

3. Those free drinks you may find on board will, if you're not careful, reward you with a fierce headache when you land. Alcohol has unpleasant side effects at high altitude.

4. Collectively, all these discomforts will intensify your jet lag symptoms at your destination.

Red eyes are recommended only for those whose schedules absolutely prevent them from picking a flight that arrives at a more sensible hour.

SUPERSONICS

Since January 1976, the Concorde (jointly built by the British and the French) has been spearing the stratosphere above the Atlantic Ocean, its waspy needle-nosed fuselage drawing crowds of gapers at airports, and its noisy takeoffs drawing crowds of angry protesters from residential neighborhoods nearby. Efficiency-minded executives always searching for new ways to extend their workdays welcomed the supersonics.

"The Concorde is a fantastic way to travel," said Robert Tisch, president of Loews Corporation. "Especially the London to New York flight," Tisch added, "which leaves at 11 A.M. and arrives at 9 A.M. It delivers me refreshed and able to pick up a day's work."

"Can you afford," asked an ad for British Airways, "to miss the chance of arriving ready for work rather than ready for bed?"

Other advertisements by Air France and its British partner in Concorde flights implied that the Concorde could, indeed, actually cut down on jet lag. Both airlines, however, soon dropped that ad theme. Scientists suggested that the crossing of five time zones, at a speed of thirteen hundred miles per hour, in three hours wouldn't eliminate the effects of jet lag, and might even compound them. It is the suddenness of time-zone shifting, they pointed out, that disrupts your inner rhythms. As far as jet lag is concerned, the supersonic traveler is no better off, say, than the subsonic transpacific clock-beater, who can perform a full day's work in Tokyo, then board a 747 nonstop to New York, arriving before the close of business that afternoon.

Nevertheless, the supersonics may reduce the travel fatigue that can make an attack of jet lag worse. Even though the Concorde's seating is more cramped than in the wide-bodied Boeing 747, the DC-10, or the Lockheed TriStar, the reduced flying time it offers is bound to be beneficial. Air France Concorde pilot Michel Butel, a fifty-nine-year-old ex–World War II fighter pilot, theorizes that fatigue reaches its apex after the passenger's fourth hour in the sky. Most Concorde flights, he points out, take between three and four hours. Not long ago, Butel departed at 7 A.M. from his home in Nice, flew to Paris, piloted the 11 A.M. Concorde to New York, and was back home in Nice, thanks to a schedule change, at 10:30 P.M.

"It was a long working day," Butel said, "but the next morning I felt just great."

PLANNING STOPOVERS

When you are choosing your flight, you should consider not only the time you want to depart and the hour at which you want to arrive, but the time the airplane takes to get to your destination. If you are traveling eastbound farther than Europe (say, to the Middle East) or farther westbound than our West Coast (say, to Australia), you may want to consider including a stopover in your itinerary. Your travel agent or airline reservations agent can probably figure out a way so that you don't have to pay extra for the privilege of spending a night or so in an in-between city.

Stopovers can help the body readjust gradually to a new time cycle and thus reduce the impact of jet lag. Birds seem to understand that fact instinctively. The Arctic tern crosses five time zones but breaks up its flight with frequent stops along the way. Again, modern man is proving to be just as clever as birds. IBM employees take a day's rest after passing through eight time zones, and Canadian government officials are entitled to a night's stopover after nine hours of flying. When President Richard Nixon embarked on his historic jaunt to China, the stops he made in

Hawaii and Guam were not, as reported, to inspect our military bases. They were for Rest and Recreation, so that he would arrive at his destination in proper working order—mentally, emotionally, and physically.

The best advice is: On any trip that takes you to the other side of the world (the worst situation for jet lag, since the more time zones you cross, the more upset your systems become), break up your journey with a one- or two-day stopover.

CHOOSING A SEAT ON BOARD

"If you are prone to motion sickness," said TV host and raconteur David Frost, "be sure you plan well ahead so that you can select a seat in the middle of the plane, right between the wings. That's where there'll probably be the least amount of that disturbing movement."

Celebrities, who spend half their lives cocooned in airplanes, have to step out of the cabin into a foreign culture ready to perform at their peak. Thus, for survival's sake, many of them soon become experts at the nuances of avoiding the discomforts of flight that can compound their jet lag. Selecting the right seat on board ranks high among their priorities.

If you are a beginner at battling jet lag, you should fire your first shot while you are booking your flight. Ask your travel agent or airline reservations agent what kind of equipment you'll be flying on. Once you know the type of airplane, you can then request a seating plan—Pan American and United are among the many airlines that publish them. If you are unable to obtain the seating plan of the particular plane you're flying on, you can get to the airport early on the day of your flight (a tactic I recommend in any case) and scan the seating plan at the airline ticket counter or at the check-in counter at your departure gate.

Either way, here are some tips culled from the celebrities and scientists:

1. If you do have a tendency toward motion sickness (discussed in detail later), select a seat in the center of the aircraft, near the forward part of the wing. That's where the ride is smoothest.

2. Choose an aisle seat; aisle seats allow you to get up and wander around, and that's beneficial, as we'll see, for your blood

circulation. An aisle seat may also allow you a little more leg room. You can extend your outer leg into the aisle, hugging the base of the seat in front of you—as long as you are careful to pull it back any time a flight attendant moves toward you. Otherwise, in a nonaisle seat, you might have to travel all the way to Europe with your toes sandwiched between the bottom of the seat in front of you and the briefcase you placed under it.

The disadvantage of an aisle seat, of course, is that other passengers will be constantly climbing over you to go to the lavatory. My policy is to bear the bruises with a smile. It's much easier on the soul to have them apologizing to you than to be imprisoned in a window seat or the center-section seats of a wide-body, refusing nature's call because you're too embarrassed to do your jungle-gym routine for the third time in two hours.

If you're traveling with a companion, he or she can select the aisle seat across from you. It makes intimate conversation a little more difficult, but that's not all bad. To combat jet lag, you want to try to relax on board as much as possible. And that gap of an aisle may act as a buffer, preventing the kinds of arguments on board that are provoked by edginess or the fear of flying.

If, however, the pain of even so slight a physical separation proves too much to bear, telephone the airline the day before you depart and ask an agent to check the availability of seats on your flight. If there are a lot of empty seats, you can gamble (after checking again when you select your seat at the gate, if you haven't done so over the telephone) and opt for a window-and-aisle combination on the same side. If your plane is not a wide-body (where aisle and window seat may be contiguous), you will have a seat between you and your companion. If no one shows up to take it, you will be able to raise both arms of that intermediary seat and cuddle up together, watching the movie as if you were snug on your living-room couch. (If you get stuck in a seat where your view of the movie is blocked, simply ask the stewardess if she can arrange a switch.)

3. If you just cannot do without a window seat, select one on the side away from the sun. They offer the best view.

4. The smoking section, as you probably have noticed, is always located at the rear of the plane. The reason is that the air-conditioning units blow from front to rear, wafting the smoke backward. Even though, in theory, the air conditioning replenishes

the air in the cabin every three minutes, you may find, in practice, more clouds hovering in the smoking section than in the stratosphere outside.

If you are a smoker, find out where the smoking section begins, and choose a seat in that row. Since the row in the front of you will be a "nonsmoker," there won't be any smoke drifting back into your face. Your own smoke will drift back to bother only those passengers behind you, who, also smokers, won't dare complain.

But what happens when your promised "smoking section" seat turns out to be in the nonsmoking area of the plane? In the days before I stopped smoking on airplanes, I was once on a flight where an irate chain smoker, positioned out of place, engaged in an ugly, loud, and ultimately futile argument with a gang of surly flight attendants.

Finally, I agreed to pocket my pack for the duration of the flight.

5. If you are a serious nonsmoker, select a seat at least four rows away from the smoking section.

6. If you are unusually tall, try to get a seat in the rows beside the emergency exits. Usually, so that people can squeeze by without getting crippled, there is more leg room than in other rows. These emergency-exit rows also offer an advantage to people who always find airplane cabins too hot: because of slight drafts from the emergency doors, these rows are often a little cooler than other parts of the plane.

7. Avoid, however, if possible, selecting a seat in the row in front of the emergency exit. In some planes, the seat backs in these rows won't fully recline.

8. If you have any kind of carry-on luggage, also avoid the rows facing the galley wall or the bulkheads. Since there will be no seats in front of you, it stands to reason that you will not be able to put, as airline regulations require on takeoff and landing, your belongings under the seat in front of you. You will have to stow your luggage overhead.

9. Avoid seats right beside the galley. Unless you're hell-bent on having an affair with a stewardess or someday becoming one yourself, such close proximity to their workplace will do nothing but fill your trip with an unending clatter. And unending chatter. When they aren't discussing their personal lives, like the rest of us, flight attendants tend to talk about the pitfalls of the job. Once

in a while you'll overhear some tibdit, about the pilot's drinking problem or the copilot's friendly Seeing Eye dog, that will make you wish you'd stayed home.

10. Unless you are physically handicapped, avoid seats near the lavatories, too. You will have crowds of people staring over your shoulder as you eat your lunch. That is, if you can eat, immersed in an ambiance of stale toilet scents.

11. If you are flying with an infant, you should choose a seat facing a bulkhead (in the front of the plane). Many airlines will then provide bassinets that clip right onto the wall in front of you. However, if you do not enjoy being serenaded by someone else's infant, bid any offer of a bulkhead seat good-bye.

12. If you are disabled in any way, selecting a seat should be a crucial part of your strategy. To begin with, for reasons of logistics many airlines restrict the number of handicapped passengers they are willing to carry aboard any particular flight. Thus, a disabled person has to be sure he finalizes his reservations far in advance of his departure date, advising the airline of his disability at the same time.

Whenever feasible, a disabled person should try to fly on a wide-body aircraft. The Boeing 747, in particular, is suitable to the handicapped person's special needs. As you enter the 747, there are three seats off the entry door. You can shift right from a wheelchair to one of these seats. Otherwise, you would have to slide onto a boarding chair, then be transported down the aisle to your seat. Wheelchairs are too wide to fit in the aisle of any commercial aircraft.

CHECKLIST OF DOS AND DON'TS

Do

- Find out what aircraft you'll be flying.
- Get a copy of its seating plan.
- Select an aisle seat.
- Stick to the center of the plane, if you are susceptible to motion sickness.
- Sit at least four rows in front of the smoking section if you are a nonsmoker.

- Sit in the first row of the smoking section if you are a smoker.
- Choose, for the seat with most leg room, one in the row beside an emergency exit.
- Choose, if you are traveling with an infant, a seat facing a bulkhead.
- Choose, if you are handicapped, a wide-body—a 747, if possible, selecting among the three seats right beside the main entry door.

Don't

- Choose a seat in the row in front of an emergency exit, next to the galley, or next to the toilets.

4

Calculating Your Jet Lag

A week or so after I began working as an airline reservations agent, my "team" moved from the day to the night shift. It wasn't long before I was overcome by some distressing symptoms. I was constantly fatigued, I couldn't sleep, my patterns of eating and elimination turned topsy-turvy. On the job, I began making errors— booking, say, a passenger on a Sunday flight that operated only Monday through Friday. If a supervisor called my attention to a mistake, I was prone to erupt in anger. Scientists, I later learned, have recognized these symptoms for a decade or so. Out of their exploration of the effects of shift work come, in part, the strategies for battling jet lag.

According to recent scientific studies, about 80 percent of all shift workers are troubled by fatigue and insomnia and malaise. It was no surprise to scientists to learn that "human error" contributed to the "accident" at the Three Mile Island nuclear power plant. That accident occurred, they point out, at 4 A.M., with a crew that had just rotated onto the night schedule. Four in the morning is very near the lowest trough in the daily, or "circadian," cycle of alertness, when your capacity to respond, say, to a warning signal is at its lowest.

"The time course of this accident strongly suggests that the operators on duty were at less than optimal phase in their individual daily performance cycles," said Dr. Charles Ehret, of the Division of Biological and Medical Research at the Argonne National Laboratories near Chicago.

Dr. Ehret and other chronobiologists have been studying the disruptive impact of time shifts. Workers in factories aren't the only endangered species. Military troops on a mission often move across time zones. So, obviously, does the pilot of your plane. And there is no specific provision in the Federal Aviation Administration regulations concerning rest time and duty time for the unpleasant realities of the twenty-four-hour sleep-wake cycle.

NASA, concerned about the well-being and performance of its orbiting astronauts, has undertaken an astonishing variety of tests. Experiments have been conducted in steel cylinders protected from the interference of magnetic fields, in Arctic locales where the sun never sets, in damp bunkers and caves where the sun never shines. The airlines themselves have borrowed some of the same tests and sophisticated telemetry used on the astronauts in space to measure the body functions of pilots and flight attendants. As a result of all this analysis and experimentation, although no one has come up with a "cure" for jet lag, scientists have developed plans that can help you suppress jet lag's worst symptoms.

But before we sift through these strategies, it's time to take a closer look at:

TIME ZONES

Standard time zones are themselves a relatively recent invention. Prior to 1883, the United States was divided, in a haphazard way, into a hundred time zones, with twenty-seven local times in the state of Michigan alone. Each local town set its clocks by the town fathers' personal best estimate of noon.

It was the railroads, with their need to predict precise arrival times across the country, that reduced those hundred U.S. time zones to the manageable number of four. In 1918 the federal government passed a law that made four time zones the standard for the entire country.

Now, the surface of the earth is divided into twenty-four zones, each of fifteen degrees latitude. The zones are numbered from 0 to 23, with "mean time" set at the Greenwich meridian—in England, not Greenwich Village or Greenwich, Connecticut.

For every fifteen degrees you move eastward (crossing one time zone) away from the Greenwich meridian, you add one hour. For every fifteen degrees you move westward, you subtract an hour. Move twelve of these time zones east or west away from the meridian, and you cross the International Date Line. If you cross the line going from east to west, you gain a day. If you cross the line going from west to east, you lose a day.

Thus, on an intercontinental flight from New York to Frankfurt, Germany (eastward), you cross five time zones—and have to add five hours (or six hours for daylight-saving time in the summer).

Below is a list of international cities you are most likely to visit. Following the name of each city is the number of hours it is ahead or behind, depending on whether your departure city is on Pacific, mountain, central, or eastern standard time. (Be sure you adjust this table to include daylight-saving time, when it is in effect, and check with your airline or travel agent to find out which other countries observe DST.)

To figure out the time difference between your departure city and your destination, add or subtract the number beside that destination city.

For instance, if you are flying from Los Angeles (Pacific time) to Oslo, Norway, add nine hours to your home time to find out what time it is in Oslo. If you are traveling from New York (eastern time) to Honolulu, subtract five hours.

City	Pacific	Mountain	Central	Eastern
Amsterdam	+ 9	+ 8	+ 7	+ 6
Anchorage	− 2	− 3	− 4	− 5
Athens	+10	+ 9	+ 8	+ 7
Auckland	+17	+16	+15	+14
Azores	+ 6	+ 5	+ 4	+ 3
Baghdad	+11	+10	+ 9	+ 8
Bangkok	+12	+11	+10	+ 9
Barcelona	+ 9	+ 8	+ 7	+ 6
Basra	+11	+10	+ 9	+ 8
Beirut	+10	+ 9	+ 8	+ 7
Berlin	+ 9	+ 8	+ 7	+ 6
Bermuda	+ 4	+ 3	+ 2	+ 1
Bombay	+13.5	+12.5	+11.5	+10.5
Brussels	+ 9	+ 8	+ 7	+ 6
Bucharest	+10	+ 9	+ 8	+ 7
Buenos Aires	+ 5	+ 4	+ 3	+ 2
Cairo	+10	+ 9	+ 8	+ 7
Calcutta	+13.5	+12.5	+11.5	+10.5
Capetown	+10	+ 9	+ 8	+ 7
Caracas	+ 4	+ 3	+ 2	+ 1

City	Pacific	Mountain	Central	Eastern
Copenhagen	+ 9	+ 8	+ 7	+ 6
Dakar	+ 8	+ 7	+ 6	+ 5
Damascus	+10	+ 9	+ 8	+ 7
Delhi	+13.5	+12.5	+11.5	+10.5
Djakarta	+15.5	+14.5	+13.5	+12.5
Dublin	+ 8	+ 7	+ 6	+ 5
Fairbanks	− 2	− 3	− 4	− 5
Frankfurt	+ 9	+ 8	+ 7	+ 6
Gander	+ 4.5	+ 3.5	+ 2.5	+ 1.5
Geneva	+ 9	+ 8	+ 7	+ 6
Glasgow	+ 8	+ 7	+ 6	+ 5
Guam	+18	+17	+16	+15
Helsinki	+10	+ 9	+ 8	+ 7
Hong Kong	+16	+15	+14	+13
Honolulu	− 2	− 3	− 4	− 5
Istanbul	+10	+ 9	+ 8	+ 7
Jerusalem	+10	+ 9	+ 8	+ 7
Johannesburg	+10	+ 9	+ 8	+ 7
Karachi	+13	+12	+11	+10
Keflavik	+ 8	+ 7	+ 6	+ 5
Kinshasa	+ 9	+ 8	+ 7	+ 6
La Paz	+ 4	+ 3	+ 2	+ 1
Lisbon	+ 9	+ 8	+ 7	+ 6
London	+ 8	+ 7	+ 6	+ 5
Madrid	+ 9	+ 8	+ 7	+ 6
Manila	+16	+15	+14	+13
Melbourne	+18	+17	+16	+15
Montevideo	+ 5	+ 4	+ 3	+ 2
Moscow	+11	+10	+ 9	+ 8
Nome	− 3	− 4	− 5	− 6
Okinawa	+17	+16	+15	+14
Oslo	+ 9	+ 8	+ 7	+ 6
Paris	+ 9	+ 8	+ 7	+ 6
Rangoon	+13.5	+12.5	+11.5	+10.5
Recife	+ 5	+ 4	+ 3	+ 2
Reykjavik	+ 8	+ 7	+ 6	+ 5
Rio de Janeiro	+ 5	+ 4	+ 3	+ 2
Rome	+ 9	+ 8	+ 7	+ 6

City	Pacific	Mountain	Central	Eastern
Saigon	+15	+14	+13	+12
Samoa	− 3	− 4	− 5	− 6
San Juan	+ 4	+ 3	+ 2	+ 1
Santiago	+ 4	+ 3	+ 2	+ 1
Seoul	+17	+16	+15	+14
Shanghai	+16	+15	+14	+13
Shannon	+ 8	+ 7	+ 6	+ 5
Singapore	+15.5	+14.5	+13.5	+12.5
Stockholm	+ 9	+ 8	+ 7	+ 6
Sydney	+18	+17	+16	+15
Tahiti	− 2	− 3	− 4	− 5
Teheran	+11.5	+10.5	+ 9.5	+ 8.5
Tokyo	+17	+16	+15	+14
Valparaiso	+ 4	+ 3	+ 2	+ 1
Vienna	+ 9	+ 8	+ 7	+ 6
Warsaw	+ 9	+ 8	+ 7	+ 6
Zurich	+ 9	+ 8	+ 7	+ 6

Armed with this chart, you can get a quick fix on approximately how long you will need to recover from jet lag at your destination. As a rough guideline, you can assume you will require twenty-four hours to adjust to each two hours of time difference. Thus, if you fly from Los Angeles (Pacific standard time) to Vienna, Austria, be prepared to suffer the throes of jet lag for about four and a half days. On the other hand, traveling from New York to California, westbound (remember: West Is Best), with a time difference of only three hours, you should be back to peak performance within a day and a half.

However, that twenty-four-hour-adjustment-period-for-every-two-hours-of-time-difference rule isn't as precise as some passengers would like. Professionals bound on business, who need to plan their activities well in advance, require a finer set of calculations. For them and for any tourist who wants to maximize his fun in some far-flung oasis, I offer the International Civil Aviation Organization's official "Jet Lag Resynchronization Formula."

HOW TO PREDICT THE DURATION OF JET LAG

Headquartered in Montreal, the International Civil Aviation Organization sends its staff on missions to the far corners of the globe. In order to predict how long it will take staff members to perform at their peak, once they arrive in the host country, ICAO experts devised the following formula: Travel time (in hours), divided by two, plus time zones in excess of four, plus departure-time coefficient, plus arrival-time coefficient equals rest period (in tenths of days).

Now, don't be turned off, as I was initially, by the complexities of the language. Even I—for whom those high-school-math rowing-against-the-current word problems were an undecipherable Rosetta Stone—even I can work this particular equation.

Just remember:

1. That you must first find out how long your flight will take.

2. That departure and arrival times in the equation are local times in both cases.

3. That those arcane-sounding "coefficients" are derived from the following table:

Departure Period	Departure Time Coefficient	Arrival Time Coefficient
8 A.M. to Noon	0	4
Noon to 7 P.M.	1	2
7 P.M. to 10 P.M.	3	0
10 P.M. to 1 A.M.	4	1
1 A.M. to 8 A.M.	3	3

Suppose, for example, you are traveling from Montreal to London—a six-hour flight. The equation would read:

$$\frac{6}{2} + 1 + 3 + 3 = \frac{10}{10} = 1$$

In other words, the ICAO would allow you one full day's rest before sending you out to perform your assignment.

Or, instead of a six-hour flight, suppose the ICAO is sending you on a twenty-six-hour one, from Montreal to Karachi, Pakistan.

How many days of leisure would you be permitted before you had to start producing results?

$$\frac{26}{2} + 5 + 4 + 3 = \frac{25}{10} = 2.5$$

Rounding off, the ICAO would allow you three days of R & R in Karachi.

However, be forewarned: Whichever method you use to compute the probable duration of your jet lag, you'll have to take into account your own age, health, and personal idiosyncrasies. Scientists have discovered that certain types of people suffer worse jet lag than others. Here are some of the personal storm warnings—and fair-weather signs—that can foul up your forecasting.

1. *The Age Factor:* The younger you are, the less jet lag will bother you. Babies under three months of age seem unaffected, while people in their sixties and older can be incapacitated for weeks. Experiments show that people in their forties to early fifties are particularly prone to having their REM sleep (that rapid-eye-movement slumber so necessary to waking up refreshed) disrupted.

2. *The Habit Factor:* "You are more likely to suffer from jet lag symptoms if you are accustomed to a rigid eating and sleeping pattern at home," said Dr. Charles Gullet, corporate director of medical services for TWA. "Pilots and other flight personnel have much less trouble adjusting," Gullet added, "because they've led a lifetime of irregular hours and erratic schedules. They are able to adapt more easily to the shift."

3. *Larks:* Early risers, who probably have natural cycles of twenty-five hours or less, may find it easier to adjust after an eastbound flight than late risers.

4. *Night Owls:* Night owls, in contrast, may have the edge when flying west; accustomed to staying up late, they can more easily absorb the stretched-out day.

Now you know, more or less, how long jet lag can incapacitate you when you arrive at your destination. But the steps you take before you board your plane can increase those dog days of discomfort—or diminish them.

5

Preadapting

The way to prevent your body from being out of sync when you arrive is to begin planning a week or so before you depart. Many scientists are convinced that the disciplined human body can adjust itself to jet lag.

"Air force pilots who fly around the world learn how to manage the problem efficiently," said Dr. Bryce Hartman, a psychologist at the Air Force School of Aerospace Medicine at Brooks Airbase, Texas. "They latch onto a mission schedule and adapt their lives to it, rather than to the rising and setting sun or to regular mealtimes."

Unfortunately, air force pilots enjoy certain advantages over us lesser mortals. My wife might object if I asked her to supply "logistical support" in the form of light-sealed living quarters and round-the-clock feeding.

Nevertheless, in a less martial manner, you can devise a mission schedule, too. It requires sacrifice and dedication, but the scientists insist that by altering your diet and sleep habits over a specific period prior to your flight, you can tune your body to a new time zone. In particular, what you eat in the days before your flight (and, as we'll learn later, during it) can determine how quickly you recover from jet lag when you land. Travelers, scientists have learned, can alter their normal diets by following certain meal plans that may fool the body into a smoother transition.

Dr. Charles Ehret, of the Argonne National Laboratories, has concocted a program to aid travelers flying east or west. Ehret's diet plans are intended to achieve rapid readjustment of the circadian rhythms. He doesn't claim that every symptom of jet lag will dissolve but that the most distressing side effects can be minimized. "Our circadian cycles are influenced by synchronizers or environmental timekeepers," explained Dr. Ehret, "such as light and darkness, alarm clocks and other social cues, and various foods, drugs, and hormones in the system."

The timekeepers crucial to Dr. Ehret's diet are certain chemicals contained in food, some of which cue the body rhythm to accelerate, others to slow it down. One of the key timekeepers is caffeine. Caffeinated beverages contain drugs called methylated xanthines, which, taken at the proper times and in the proper amounts, can help speed up your biological clock by several hours. Speeding up your internal clock is beneficial when traveling east, when the day-night cycle also quickens.

THE ARGONNE CLOCKWATCHER'S AND WORLD TRAVELER'S DIET

Eastbound

Dr. Ehret's plan requires eastbound travelers to begin modifying their diets four days before they depart. It demands enough self-discipline on the part of the passenger to alternate periods of all-out feasting with periods of relative fasting.

Suppose, for example, you are going to fly from Boston to Athens, which means that you will cross seven time zones and have to move your watch seven hours ahead. Let's say that you will be departing on a Wednesday. According to the Ehret plan, Sunday and Tuesday would be your "feast" days: You gorge yourself on large meals. On Monday and Wednesday, in contrast, you "fast"— limiting your intake to light foods. The aim of this diet is to orchestrate the chronotype enzymes of the body's cells so that they all shift together into the required (at your destination) rhythm.

On the first day of the four-day diet plan, you begin with a heaping high-protein breakfast, then follow up with an equally high-protein lunch. That evening you indulge yourself in a high-carbohydrate dinner. On the second day of the diet, you "fast"— consuming only three light meals. You repeat this pattern again on days three and four.

The idea behind seesawing from proteins to carbohydrates is that protein intake stimulates mental activity, while the carbohydrates induce sleepiness, easing the circadian rhythm into the new eastern time sequence.

On the departure day, disciples of the Ehret eastbound plan should avoid imbibing any caffeinated beverages at breakfast and avoid consuming any carbohydrates (which bring on sleepiness) until 6 P.M. (We are supposing here an evening departure.) Between the time the plane departs and midflight, dieters drink three or four cups of black coffee or strong tea (no sugar or cream, please) to assist in phase advancement. The caffeine will speed up the internal clock to more closely match that of the new time zone.

On board the airplane, Dr. Ehret advises passengers to refrain from eating any food at all until the "breakfast" meal. You should skip the movie, stay away from bright lights and lively discussions until the time comes to break your fast, just before you arrive at your destination. A half-hour or so before you are scheduled to land, you turn on your overhead light, stretch, walk about, perform some in-seat exercises, and start chatting with anyone who isn't too groggy or grumpy. Then eat a high-protein and high-calorie meal to replenish the energy reserves of what by now should be a fairly well depleted liver—one in approximate sync with the livers of the local populace.

The first day at your destination, eat a hearty lunch and heavy dinner, when the natives do. Then go to bed early, and continue on the local time schedule.

Westbound

In the Ehret plan, to prepare for a westbound flight, you follow the same four-day feast-and-fast routine. The difference between the eastbound and westbound diets comes on the day you depart.

Whereas eastbound you avoided caffeinated beverages on the morning of your departure, westbound Ehret recommends that you drink a lot of coffee or tea before noon. The caffeine will keep you active for prolonged periods and give you the illusion of a longer day. After noontime, however, caffeinated beverages are forbidden. Alcoholic drinks should also be avoided that afternoon and evening.

On board the airplane, you switch to caffeinated drinks. And now, during the flight, if you can't restrain yourself, you may drink an alcoholic beverage. Alcohol has the effect of slowing down your internal clock, helping to readjust it to the time zone of your destination. But remember: It's far easier to get a hangover in a high-flying jet than in your local saloon. Two drinks in the air may have the impact of three at sea level.

The Ehret plans call for an amount of will power many of us simply cannot muster. Yet, despite their demands, the diets may be the best solution for athletes, business executives, and others who are determined (or obligated) to spend their first few days away from home in top mental and physical shape. Other inveterate travelers have devised their own personal plans.

"I go on a diet a week before takeoff, eating the bare minimum," said Jim Arey, director of corporate public relations for Pan Am. Arey adheres to this ascetic routine even on prolonged trips, such as the fifteen-hour marathon from New York to Tokyo. "Although I try not to eat," Arey added, "I make sure I drink lots of fluids— but no alcohol. I feel fit as a fiddle when I arrive and only require eight to twelve hours of sleep the first night."

While Arey's fast makes *him* feel good, there's no scientific evidence it will work for you. If you aren't well motivated enough to suffer through the Ehret plan's four days of feasting and fasting, you can attempt to adapt your body to your new time zone by gradually shifting your sleeping and eating habits.

BEDTIME-AND-MEAL SHIFTS

In a sense, insomniacs suffer from a daily "jet lag." Scientists have learned that, instead of operating on a twenty-four-hour cycle of hormonal excretions and highs and lows of body temperature, many insomniacs have cycles that run anywhere from twenty to twenty-eight hours. Chronotherapists at sleep clinics across the country are learning how to set back or forward insomniac body clocks that run too fast or too slow. At the Stanford University Sleep Clinic, for instance, patients who can't seem to fall asleep till the early hours of the morning gradually get trained to move their own inner time-pieces back. In gradual shifts, each lasting a few nights, insomniacs retard their bedtimes from, say, 5 P.M. to 4 A.M. to 3 A.M., etc.

The jet traveler can employ the same technique.

If you're traveling west, for two days before your flight postpone the time you usually go to bed by two or three hours. If you're traveling east, try to retire a couple of hours earlier. Your body clock won't be fully adapted to the new time cycle when you land, but you will have made a start in the right direction.

At the same time, you can also start shifting your meal times in the direction of those of your destination city.

The liability of these bedtime and mealtime changes, of course, is that you may, especially if you attempt the tactic over too long a period, encounter the malaise and fatigue and insomnia endemic among shift workers in factories. The experiment can also backfire because of other complications. While you are re-regulating your body clock to coincide with the foreign night-day cycle, everyone around you will be sticking to good old U.S.A. time.

"I tried a meal shift one week in advance," recalled Dr. Monte Buchsbaum of the National Institute of Mental Health. "On the day of the departure, I ate early and flew into New York to connect with an evening flight, which was delayed three hours. There I was," Dr. Buchsbaum added, "ready for dinner at 4 P.M. (stomach time), with all the airport restaurants closed."

PLANNING YOUR ACTIVITIES AHEAD

I'll discuss in detail in a later chapter the dos and don'ts of scheduling your activities during your first few days abroad. But be forewarned, especially if you are traveling on business: Don't plan any crucial conferences or important appointments on the same day after a flight with a time shift of several or more hours, particularly if you are heading east. And beware of anyone traveling abroad empowered to make a deal for you. One jet-setting U.S. management consultant revealed that while his company's regulations prevent *him* from concluding, after a flight across time zones, any deal involving his own firm's funds, those regulations *do not* prohibit him from committing the hard-earned cash of a client.

Later, I'll have more to say about preadapting your own scheduling, when on business or holiday, to the schedules of your foreign hosts. I'll offer some suggestions on how to reset your body clock to local time and how to take tactical advantage of the disparity between your internal clock and the external one at your destination. But is all this planning—the dieting, the meal shifts— truly necessary? Isn't there some magic potion you can take to turn back or forward the hands of your infernal internal time-piece? The answer is, absolutely—not yet.

AN ANTI–JET LAG ANTIDOTE

Aside from caffeine, which can help speed up your body clock, and alcohol, which can help slow it down, medicine has yet to discover any safe substance (and alcohol is not "safe" at elevated altitudes) able to aid in your adjustment to a new time zone. However, some promising discoveries in one field of medicine may eventually produce just such a panacea. Oddly enough, the good news comes not from the aeromedical specialists or the chronobiologists. The ultimate weapon to wipe out circadian dys-rhythmia may come from the psychiatrists.

Some psychiatrists, it seems, have noted similarities between the symptoms a traveler experiences after jetting across too many time zones and the symptoms of patients suffering from severe depression. Like jet-laggers, patients with depressive conditions show disturbances in the timing of their sleep: They wake up with depression at its worst in the early morning and show ab-normalities in the daily rhythm of their hormone secretions. If this connection between circadian dysrhythmia and depression is a valid one, are there drugs useful in treating depression that would also help the jet traveler?

Going eastbound, encountering short days and short nights, you would need a drug that could speed up your body clock. In a recent clinical study, conducted by the National Institute of Mental Health, psychiatrist Thomas Wehr and some colleagues managed just such a feat. By prescribing dosages of an antidepressant called impramine (brand name Tofranil, both in the United States and in most countries abroad), Dr. Wehr was able to bring temporary relief to a depressed manic-depressive woman by shifting her sleep period so that she awoke six hours earlier than usual. If you could take, before you departed, a drug that would advance your body clock six hours, you would arrive, say, in London (departing from New York) in tune with native time. Reportedly, impramine has been used by some pilots, on an experimental basis, to achieve just such an effect.

But suppose you are traveling to the west. Facing the prospect of longer days and nights, you want a drug capable of slowing down your body clock, not speeding it up. Lithium carbonate (trade names Lithane or Eskalith in the United States), another antidepressant used to help manic-depressive patients, seems to have just that effect.

The problem is that these drugs are powerful medicines, capable of doing as much damage as they do good. Unless carefully monitored, impramine can induce blurred vision, headaches, dizziness, and constipation. It can give you a skin rash, damage your liver and bone marrow, and make it difficult for you to urinate. Likewise, lithium carbonate can engender nausea, diarrhea, weakness, and tremors. Under no conditions should either of these drugs be taken without a doctor's prescription, and currently, the medical profession sees no reason to prescribe them for jet lag at all—not, at least, in their present, potent forms.

If they can be safely adapted for more general use, the initial beneficiaries are likely to be those individuals for whom jet lag isn't a temporary inconvenience but a definite liability, such as the pilot of your plane, facing the prospect of having to land the aircraft in a dense fog after crossing eight disruptive time zones.

Widely prescribing such drugs as antidotes to jet lag "would be like killing a fly with a sledgehammer," warned Dr. Henry Masur of the International Health Care Service of New York Hospital. "I don't consider the use of such drugs as lithium to be practical in this case."

So, for the time being at least, you'll have to forget the idea of discovering any elixir to end jet lag instantly. But even if you can't slay this monster, by making careful preparations in advance of your flight, you can still outwit it.

6

Airplane Meals

It wasn't the chicken cordon bleu, smothered in a sauce that smelled like ammonia, that turned me off airline food once and for all, or the steak as tough as shoe leather, or the vegetables dappled with dewy ice crystals. What killed my appetite for airborne meals was a simple slice of hard-boiled egg.

I was traveling on business to California, with a pair of companions sitting beside me. A flight attendant had just served us our luncheon trays. My companions were picking at selected morsels, slicing off tidbits as cautiously as a surgeon operating on some vital organ. Meanwhile, I was wolfing down my entrée. I always did. I ate anything any airline stewardess set in front of me. If, instead of roast beef, she had lifted the cover off my plate to reveal a building brick smothered in Three-in-One oil, I would have asked for a hammer and chisel and gnawed on that, too.

By the time I was three-quarters through my slice of roast beef, my companions had pushed away their trays, virtually untouched. I was raising my fork to spear the slice of hard-boiled egg in my salad dish, when my friend in the seat next to me placed his hand on my arm. "I'll show you something very odd," he said. Then he lifted, with the side of his knife, my slice of egg out of my salad dish, depositing it in a clearing on his own plate. Carefully, he fitted first his own egg slice, then the egg slice of our companion, on top of mine. "Do you see what I mean?" he said.

I looked straight down: The three thin egg slices had melded into one thick one. All three slices, it seemed, were exactly the same size.

"Have you ever, in your life, seen three eggs exactly the same size?" the friend asked.

I had to admit that I had not.

"Neither," he replied, "has any hen."

My friend explained that, owing to the need to have every item on your tray virtually identical in size to every item on everyone else's tray (not to keep you from complaining about your neighbor's larger portion but so that all this prepackaged food can slide into narrow galley storage shelves) the egg slices are prefabricated ones. The egg isn't synthetic; it's simply reconstituted at the processing plant. There, eggs are shelled, then the white is separated from the yolk. Machines cook the white in identically shaped rings and cook the yolk in identically sized centers. Then the yolk is reinserted into the white—and you have your slice of hard-boiled egg.

Somehow I haven't been able to eat an airplane meal since.

"There's no such thing as a good airline anymore," said Morley Safer of "60 Minutes." Safer travels eleven months and logs more than two hundred thousand miles each year. "They deteriorated when they started advertising how good they were." Safer never flies without a pepper mill, a bottle of Dijon mustard—and lots of antacid.

It isn't that the airlines don't try to provide savory meals. The quality of the food itself is high, and the airlines go to extraordinary lengths to ensure that their menus are varied. You'll find fresh fish and tropical fruit on your trays. First-class passengers may even get caviar. In a recent year TWA served more than sixteen million airborne meals. At an average of ten dollars a head in economy class and often twice that much for first-class fare, you can't say the airlines aren't trying.

The problem with airline food lies elsewhere. The meals have to be precooked, then frozen, then defrosted in microwave ovens on board for thirty seconds before they are served to you. (Usually, the only items cooked on the plane are prebrowned steaks, in ovens powered by the airplane engines.) You get powdered milk or half-and-half to lighten your coffee because fresh milk turns sour in a pressurized cabin. Your entrée has to be some concoction easily cut with a plastic knife and fork, and stable enough to stab and guide into your mouth. The menu, like network television programs, has to be bland enough to satisfy almost everybody— which means few spices or savory sauces. Airline food isn't bad, but it *is* boring. And even worse, although you don't have to take precautions, as your pilot does, against ptomaine poisoning (usually each of the crew members in the cockpit is served a different meal), your onboard meals may contribute to a severe case of jet lag.

According to Dr. F. S. Preston, Deputy Director of Medical Services of British Airways, many of the symptoms commonly attributed to jet lag may simply be the result of eating too much of the wrong kind of food during a flight. Some tips you should follow when confronted by an airline meal are:

1. *Pass up foods that form gases—beans, cabbage, onions, raw apples, cucumbers, and melons—and foods cooked in fat.* At airplane cabin pressure, the gas and fat may turn your belly into a boiler.

2. *Eat very little.* "On ground, I get a lot of flack about how blah airline food is," said one veteran TWA flight attendant. "But in the air, for every complaint about the food, I get twenty passengers who not only finish everything on their trays, but who want a little compliment for doing it. And many passengers who do leave food apologize," she added. "It seems many people have a compulsion to eat everything put in front of them."

Some passengers try to justify the gluttony that overwhelms them in the air by claiming that eating a large meal helps them fall asleep. According to a pamphlet prepared by the medical department of Pan Am, however, large meals do *not* make you sleepy. You doze off faster, and sleep more soundly, when your stomach is not stuffed.

3. *Eat very cautiously.* When the pilot's voice comes piping over the loudspeaker predicting turbulence ahead, it's time not only to fasten your seat belt but to button your lips. If God had intended you to eat while bouncing up and down, He would have put a pogo stick in the back of your pants.

4. *Obey the bidding of your "stomach clock."* The airlines serve meals at times convenient to their busy flight attendants. Unless you have been gradually adapting your mealtimes to some prearranged schedule, in the air, as much as possible, you should try to match your mealtimes with the time your "stomach clock" is used to eating. If you are departing in the early evening, for example, and your meal on board won't be served till some time later than your normal dinner hour, snack at the airport before you get on the plane.

5. *Don't chew gum.* Gum chewing results in your swallowing a lot of air. Most of us are already too full of hot air.

6. *Pass up any rich and exotic dishes.* Resist sampling any dish with a foreign name, which you haven't tried before, till you land. Especially avoid foreign foods on foreign airlines. They may contain spices that send you sprinting toward the lavatory. Again, wait until you are on terra firma before you indulge in the local cuisine.

7. *Best of all, pass up the airline meals completely.* Most pasengers don't eat because they are hungry, but because they are bored or just plain scared.

"I eat without stop," said comedienne Joan Rivers. "They just leave the hors d'oeuvres tray with me. "I am not," she added, "going down dieting."

BROWN-BAGGING IT

Now that aeromedical experts equate what we eat, and when we eat it, with jet lag, jet-setters are turning their traditional disdain for airline meals into an excuse to bring on board their favorite delicacies. This chic trend toward carrying into the airplane food that satisfies both scientists and gourmets is one you should mimic. Days before your flight, you should have purchased a small picnic basket. The day you depart, fill it with all those goodies you've always craved on an airplane but couldn't obtain.

"My husband and I always 'brown-bag' it," said chef Julia Child. "We've been doing it for years. We don't have those terrific New York delis to draw on," added Child, who resides in a small town in Massachusetts, "so we just take whatever's left around—leftover lamb, sometimes tuna fish—generally in sandwiches." Since she resents paying for food she doesn't eat, Child is particularly enamored of no-frills flights. However, if airlines insist on serving meals, she said, "I don't see why they just don't serve really marvelous sandwiches, too."

Other gourmets opt for the silver-platter, rather than brownbag, approach. Gloria Swanson and her husband, gourmand William Dufty, bring their food on board in a variety of carryalls that sometimes include traditional Japanese lunch baskets. They also take along their own utensils and lightweight lacquered serving plates.

"Madame fixes the cold dishes; I do the cooked ones," Dufty explained. Their favorite carry-on snacks are cold cooked rice and vegetables, pâté, all kinds of salads, and thermoses full of lentil and pea soups.

More and more, jet-setting rebels against routine airline food are filling insulated bags and thermoses with such treats as caviar, cold lobster, Virginia ham, and even chicken soup—as crucial a culinary security blanket for jet-laggers as for sufferers of more mundane afflictions.

Westbound from Europe, said Craig Claiborne, "I raid the excellent in-town and airport gourmet shops and bring on board delicious pâtés and cold meats and pastries and breads." While his less adventurous fellow-travelers are gagging over their half-thawed quiche, Claiborne is lusting over roast quail wrapped in bacon.

Seventeen-year-old tennis star Andrea Jaeger spends a great deal of time doing hard-time on inter- and transcontinental airline flights. In 1981 alone, she had to invest a formidable forty-six thousand dollars in economy-class fares. Nevertheless, like Craig Claiborne, Jaeger refuses the airline food, preferring the items she carries aboard: fresh fruit she sneaks through customs.

If enough people desert airline cuisine there may yet be min-iaturized picnic baskets. And Louis Vuitton might even design an insulated version of its already renowned brown bag.

CHECKLIST OF DOS AND DONT'S:

Do

- Purchase a picnic basket and brown-bag your airborne dinner.
- Eat lightly while in the air.
- Eat cautiously if the pilot warns you're going to be plowing through some turbulence.
- Tell the flight attendant to take back that tray of food.

Don't

- Pack any beans, cabbage, onions, raw apples, cucumbers, or melons in that pretty picnic basket.
- Bring on board greasy foods.
- Eat anything exotic or rich.
- Chew gum.

7

Science, as we have seen, has yet to discover any safe, specific medication to alleviate the symptoms of jet lag or to eliminate it. But that doesn't mean that American airplane passengers are padlocking their medicine cabinets before they start packing. In a recent survey of transcontinental travelers, and travelers jetting from the East Coast to Europe, just under 50 percent of the people questioned admitted taking one or more medications during the flight or during the two hours prior to departure. More than a third of those travelers said they took medication specifically because they were flying—mostly sleeping pills, tranquilizers, antihistamines, and anti-motion-sickness prescriptions. The rest took medication unrelated to their trip—antibiotics, insulin, antihypertensives, and birth-control pills.

The problem is that, in an airplane cabin, some of those pills can turn nasty on you; often, there are ways of dealing with some minor ailment in the air that are just as effective but don't involve risky side effects that can complicate your jet lag when you land.

People who do have to take medication at regular times because of some chronic condition may find that jet lag itself—the speeding up or slowing down of their internal body clocks—introduces an unknown integer into the delicate equation underlying their continued good health. Pregnant women, in particular, should avoid taking medication unless it is prescribed by their physicians.

What should you do when you are faced with a long flight across several time zones and are suffering from a cold, or are taking an oral birth-control pill, or are a diabetic? The answer you choose may contribute to jet lag—or decrease it. In any case, you will have to prepare your own personal medicine kit *before* you depart. Flight attendants are trained to provide emergency medical assistance when absolutely necessary, and every airplane has its own well-stocked medical kit. But commercial airplanes aren't drugstores. Your demand for a nasal spray on board will probably be met with a stony glare. The stewardess will offer you some tissues. And if that doesn't satisfy you and if she's harried or edgy from overwork, she might just suggest you roll down your shirt-sleeve and use that.

Remember: No one is immune to jet lag. What you are trying to do is to avoid any complications that will make your suffering worse.

YOUR MEDICAL KIT

Long before you start packing that set of yellow American Tourister luggage you bought at a bargain, you should be planning what to put in the smallest, but the most crucial, "suitcase" of all. Anyone who takes a long jet flight should carry a personal medical kit. Don't pack it away in your luggage; bring it onto the plane. If you don't bring a medication you need with you, you are not going to get it on board. Furthermore, you may not be able to obtain it when you land either.

Consider a medication as commonplace as aspirin. If you want a bottle of aspirin abroad, you have to ask for: Ascriptin in Mexico; Dispril in Belgium, Switzerland, Norway, the Netherlands, and Sweden; Neutracetyl in France; Andol in Yugoslavia; Butacyl in Israel; Trineral ovaltabletten in West Germany . . . get the point? In the major capitals around the world, you won't have much difficulty finding a *farmaceutico,* or a "chemist," who recognizes the elixir you need by its American brand name. In the suburban or rural backwaters, however, when buying medicine, you'd better learn the local word for "stomach pump" as well.

When I travel, as my "medicine kit" I use the soft plastic carrying bag my old electric razor came in. If you have a camera cover you're not going to use, that will do, too—although, in case of spills, kits that zip shut are preferable to kits that snap. Cosmetic bags are appropriate, too—as long as you have someplace else to store the makeup and moisturizers you're taking with you.

What do you put in that medicine kit? That is a question you should decide with your family doctor, depending on your health and your habits. As a guide, though, here are some suggestions.

The medical department of Aer Lingus, for example, makes up a medical kit for the use of its employees when they are traveling. The kit itself is very small, measuring only six inches by two inches by two inches. Yet it contains what Aer Lingus considers the essential drugs useful for most minor maladies. Some of the items in the Aer Lingus kit require a doctor's prescription.

For Headache: Panadol tablets (Tylenol, Tempra, or Datril in the U.S.).

Indigestion: Bisodol tablets. (After thorough testing of U.S. brand-name products, Consumer Union's medical consultants recommend antacids containing aluminum and magnesium, such as Maalox. And, again, pregnant women beware: You should check with your doctor before taking any antacids, some of which may contain large amounts of sodium or aspirin.)

Infection or Fever: Any simple antibiotic your doctor thinks appropriate.

Travel sickness: Kwells (Dramamine is a similar over-the-counter medication in the U.S.)

Diarrhea: Streptotriad tablets. (Ask your doctor to prescribe a U.S. equivalent.)

Insomnia: Dalmane tablets.

To this list, Dr. Helmut Baark, chief medical officer of Lufthansa German Airlines, adds the following items:

- An assortment of Band-Aids and muslin bandages—say, three each of five, four, three, and two inches.
- An antiseptic.
- A small pair of pointed scissors.
- A pair of tweezers for splinters.
- Aralen or Resochin, for travelers visiting malarial regions.
- A penicillin preparation (prescribed by your physician) if you are going to an area where you won't be able to contact a doctor for three or four days (if, of course, you aren't allergic to penicillin).
- A supply of cough drops.
- An antiallergic ointment that stops itching from insect bites.
- A thermometer in a metal case.

- A foot powder, if you plan to walk a lot or hike. (Your foot powder should be one, Dr. Baark recommends, with an antimycosis—antifungus—effect, since mycoses have been on the increase in recent years. After bathing, he advises, whether at a beach or a swimming pool, always lie on your own towel or bathrobe—never simply on the ground, at the edge of the pool, or in a deck chair.)
- Also, I would suggest including a nasal decongestant.

Some of these medications you definitely won't need until after you land. With luck, you won't need to use most of them at all. Others you may need to use during the flight—I'll discuss when and how later. However, some medications, in order to have any effect, must be taken *before you depart*.

MOTION SICKNESS

In the early 1950s, when I took my first flight—with my mother, from Buffalo to Boston to visit a relative who was ill—the first thing every traveler did was to reach into the pocket on the seatback in front of him and make sure there was a special plastic-lined bag, in case he was forced to suddenly review the contents of his last meal during the flight. The airplanes were small, the cabin air comparatively polluted. At lower altitudes, any encounter with turbulence left you feeling as if you'd just tried to cross the Atlantic on a rubber raft.

Even if you were able to resist the erratic motion of the airplane, the unsettling music of many passengers around you violently wretching, and reaching for their bags, was enough to start your stomach vibrating in distressing symmetry.

Nowadays, of course, the behemoths that ply the airways across continents and oceans are almost completely pressurized, the air inside them cleaned every three minutes, while they soar through air so rarefied that most turbulence is left rumbling thousands of feet below. Still, though, even a flight on a jumbo jet can occasionally get rough—that's why smart travelers always keep their seat belts loosely fastened, whether the warning sign is flashing or not. And even without rough weather, a considerable percentage of air travelers are susceptible to motion sickness. Whenever your plane is held up in air traffic and starts circling, what's in your stomach is liable to start revolving, too. The culprit is the fluid in the canals of your inner ear, where your sense of balance is located. Even if you don't have a chronic malfunction of this balancing mechanism, certain kinds of movements of your head can send a message to your stomach, telling it to start feeling queasy.

Drugs

The key thing to remember about medications for motion sickness is: *You have to take them before you embark on your flight, since once you start feeling those unpleasant symptoms, they won't work.*

As for which particular drug to choose—consult your family doctor. There is a virtual supermarketful of antinausea medications available, but the drugs most often called on to aid chronic sufferers of motion sickness belong to the family of antihistamines. The easiest to obtain, because they require no prescription, are:

1. Cyclizine: brand name Marezine in the U.S. and most European countries; in Great Britain the trade name is Valoid.
2. Meclizine: brand name Bonine in the U.S.
3. Dimenhydrinate: brand name Dramamine in the U.S., Mexico, and most of Europe.

However, despite the fact that these medicines can be purchased over the counter in the U.S., I repeat: Consult your doctor before deciding to take them. They can make you sleepy; they can even affect your motor coordination. If, when you land, you plan to go straight to your hotel or to spend a leisurely day strolling around, these drugs might be suitable for your motion sickness. But if you weren't able to avoid scheduling that important business conference on your first day abroad, sit in your airplane seat and suffer. Losing your company's money in a deal may be more dangerous to your health than losing your lunch. For severe cases of motion sickness, of course, there are stronger drugs.

Most of our astronauts had spent their professional lives, before cruising into space, as test pilots. Despite the fact that they passed their days coasting upside down at Mach 2 speed, or turning their experimental aircraft like tops, or plummeting straight down toward the earth, most of them had never experienced motion sickness. But spinning around the earth turned out to be another story. Even more embarrassing, a couple of these daredevils got motion sickness *after* they returned to earth—bobbing up and down in the sea in their capsules.

To combat their motion sickness, scientists prescribed for the astronauts dosages of scopolamine combined with Dexedrine. The problem for the ordinary traveler is that both of these drugs have severe side effects and are therefore—rightly—only obtainable with a doctor's prescription. The only people who should consider taking them are professionals who need to be free of motion sickness to provide the rest of us with some vital service.

Fighting Motion Sickness Without Drugs

Unless you are a habitual victim of motion sickness—in the air, in a car, or at sea—you shouldn't have to worry about it, since today's inter- and transcontinental aircraft are so stable. If, however, you do even occasionally suffer some of the symptoms during flights, you should take advantage of these tips:

1. Avoid eating fried or fatty foods.
2. Choose a seat between the wings.
3. Don't drink alcohol.
4. And when the dreaded syndrome starts:
   a) Avoid reading.
   b) Don't look at the horizon.
   c) Recline your seat-back as far as possible.
   d) Keep your eyes closed.
   e) Loosen your clothes as much as possible.
   f) Point the air-blower overhead directly at your face.

Drugs and Drinking

Before you decide to take any medication (especially if you don't really have to on doctor's orders) prior to your flight, remember that you may have to pass up that bon voyage cocktail. Of the five medications most commonly associated with air travel, only aspirin does *not* seem to interact with alcohol. The other four—

antihistamines, tranquilizers, sleeping and motion-sickness preparations (close relatives of antihistamines)—if taken while alcohol is present in the body, may produce what doctors call a "synergistic" effect. In other words, the impact of the alcohol plus the medicine may be greater than the effect of each alone. One plus one equals three, or even four.

Mixing drugs and drinking can cause—in the air much quicker than on land—your thinking to cloud up and your coordination to turn clumsy. It can induce all the symptoms of a classic hangover: drowsiness, fatigue, dizziness, headaches, and increased reaction time.

TRAVELING WITH A COLD

One other minor ailment deserves your attention before you depart. During your flight, a minor cold can prove to be a major pain in the . . . ear. For reasons I'll discuss later, when I reveal some methods of relieving the pressure without using medicines, when the plane is taking off or landing, you may develop an earache. If you have a cold, the odds in favor of your feeling pain increase. So, if you do have a cold, be sure to pack that decongestant in your medical kit. There are many effective ones on the market—inhalers, tablets, sprays, and drops.

Whichever form of decongestant you select, use it right before you board the plane and, again, as soon as the pilot or flight attendant announces that you are about to begin descending toward your destination.

8

Special Advice for Special People

In one grueling three-week period, in the spring of 1982, fifty-seven-year-old Secretary of State Alexander M. Haig flew nearly thirty thousand intercontinental air miles, to limit the bloodshed between Great Britain and Argentina over the Falkland Islands. In one eight-day period alone Haig could have adjusted his wristwatch twenty-two times. Haig concluded one eighteen-hour flight from Argentina by plunging into eleven straight hours of negotiations with British officials. The *London Daily Mirror* trumpeted: HOW MUCH MORE CAN HAIG'S HEART STAND? Two years before, in 1980, Haig had undergone triple coronary bypass surgery.

For some inter- and transcontinental travelers, the conditions in an airplane cabin—and that special condition of modern air travel called jet lag—can mean more than a temporary nuisance. They can be a matter of life or death.

Aeromedical specialists know that the heart undergoes a series of reactions during intercontinental air travel. There may be a rise in levels of stress hormones—noradrenaline and adrenaline, as well as fatty triglycerides. There is the increase in ozone, the lowered air pressure in an airplane cabin, the stress of takeoffs and landings, the stretches of prolonged inactivity in between—all these factors may act to alter heart rate and blood pressure.

Dr. W. Gerald Austen, chief of surgery at Massachusetts General Hospital, told *Time* magazine that Haig was in no real danger at all. "Patients who have successful coronary bypass surgery have very good blood flow restored to the heart," said Dr. Austen, who performed such an operation on another former secretary of state, Henry Kissinger. "It is not surprising that those patients can do anything that any other healthy person can do."

However, people with heart conditions—and diabetics and women taking oral contraceptives—should (indeed, may have to) take special precautions and devote considerable time to planning their air trips, or else they may arrive less healthy than when they departed.

HEART PATIENTS

Generally speaking, the aeromedical specialists say, if a patient can walk a hundred yards and climb twenty steps without distress, he is fit to fly in a pressurized aircraft. There are, however, limiting factors.

1. A patient who has suffered an acute coronary condition within the past four weeks should be advised not to fly, unless his cardiologist can satisfy the airline's medical department that the flight won't affect the patient's condition. The problem is that high altitudes can be harmful to someone with a cardiovascular condition, and inside the airplane cabin the altitude is just about the same as, say, that of Denver, Colorado—about seven thousand feet. If your doctor doesn't want you to go to a Denver or a Mexico City, you shouldn't be flying in a long-distance commercial jet at all.

2. Patients with pacemakers can fly, because the pacemaker in no way interferes with or will be affected by the electronic equipment of the aircraft. However, pacemaker patients should not pass through the metal-detection units installed at airports for security purposes. Some of those units are capable of interfering with a pacemaker.

Along with these few limitations, the aeromedical specialists offer the following advice:

- Carry your most recent electrocardiogram with you, as well as a complete set of instructions covering the implantation of your pacemaker and its potential functional problems.
- Find out the altitude at your destination, and at any stopovers you plan to make en route.

- If you need to take any medicine, make sure you carry it with you. It won't do you much good if it's in the airplane's cargo bay.
- Before you leave, ask your doctor to give you the name of a hospital capable of treating your ailment, in every city you plan to visit. Doctors know, or can find out, which hospitals—at home or abroad—offer adequate services and which ones don't. Your doctor may also be able to give you the name of a colleague abroad, in each country, who has a reputation for being competent.

DIABETES

Cardiovascular patients have to be concerned with the debilitating effects of travel fatigue and the special environmental conditions in the cabin of a high-flying airplane. However, jet lag itself—the shortening of the day traveling eastbound, its lengthening on a westbound journey—poses for them no particular dangers. For the more than ten million Americans who suffer from diabetes, however, circadian dysrhythmia can disrupt the rigid routine of meals and medication so necessary to their health. To avoid risks and complications, diabetics need to plan ahead, beginning their special preparations on the day they purchase their tickets.

Diabetic Meals

If you are a diabetic, you know that a special diet is crucial for maintaining your health. Fortunately, virtually every commercial airliner is willing to cater to your needs. When I was an airline reservations agent, for instance, and a passenger told me he was a diabetic, I would punch into my computer terminal a code assuring him of a special meal in the air.

Be sure you request your diabetic meal when you make your reservation—or, at the latest, when you purchase your airline tickets. Some airlines stock standard diabetic menus. Other commercial carriers will ask you what you usually eat (for breakfast or lunch or dinner—depending on the time of departure, and the type of meal served to your fellow passengers) and will try to duplicate that diet.

However, when you board the airplane, you have to pay special attention. Sometimes the flight attendants know that someone on board has ordered a special diabetic meal, but they may not know which passenger or where he is sitting. To avoid having your condition blared over the airplane loudspeaker, you should identify yourself to a flight attendant as soon as you enter the airplane cabin.

According to a friend of mine who is both a diabetic and a frequent traveler, airline diabetic meals tend to be just as bland and unappetizing as those offered to other passengers. He saves himself some worry—What happens if the diabetic meal doesn't get loaded onto the plane?—and some will power—How will he force himself to eat the meal if it does arrive at his seat?—by taking the advice of celebrity jet-setters, and brown-bagging it. He carries his own meals on board the airplane.

Medication

Some diabetics control their condition by diet alone; apart from getting the right food at the right times during their flights, jet travel across several time zones presents them with no extraordinary problems. It's diabetics on a strict regimen of medication who have to do some clever calculating before they embark on a flight. If you are traveling westbound or eastbound across our own continent, or to another one, your day is either going to be longer than usual (west) or shorter (east). Thus, you have to change not only the times you take your medication, but, perhaps, the strength of individual dosages. Anyone on a twenty-four-hour medication cycle faces this dilemma. What compounds the problem for diabetics is that their medication is linked to mealtimes, which will be altered, too.

Until recently, says Dr. Helmut Baark of Lufthansa, passengers were advised to take along a second watch and then to take their shots or medicine as usual according to the time at home. But this system led to complications. "First, the time for taking the medicine at the arrival place might fall in the middle of the night," said Dr. Baark. "Second, following the original schedule would become completely unphysiological after a few days, since the person will have adjusted to the new day-night rhythm."

Now, aeromedical specialists recommend more subtle schedule shifts for diabetics who control their illness with medication, depending on the kind of insulin they take and the duration and direction of their journey. *You should work out your own particular schedule in consultation with your doctor; he or she knows your medical history and how well you are able to control your condition.* However, as a guideline, here are some tips on how to telescope or stretch your own twenty-four-hour medication cycle to match the circadian dysrhythmia you'll encounter en route to jet lag.

First, determine whether you are flying away from the sun and with time (westbound) or into the sun and against time (eastbound.) Consult the time-difference chart on pages 29–31. A minus number next to your destination city means you will be gaining hours; a plus number means that you will be losing hours.

Westbound: Travelers who take insulin don't need special schedules when flying, say, from New York to California. The flights generally leave in the morning or very early afternoon, arriving in the afternoon or early evening. You will have crossed only three time zones, and you can readjust your meal and medication schedule without much difficulty.

It's when you fly from New York to Honolulu, say, or to Tokyo, that things become complicated. These flights involve five- to fourteen-hour time changes and may force you to modify your mealtimes and insulin schedules. The British Diabetic Association recommends that if you are flying across four or more time zones westbound (adding four or more hours to your day), you should:

1. Step up your insulin dosage by 10 percent, if you customarily take one shot of the "intermediate"-type insulin each day.

2. Add a third injection—just before you consume the extra meal you'll eat in flight—to the two you normally take, if your usual schedule specifies a dosage of regular-type insulin (or a blend of regular and intermediate) every morning and evening. That extra shot should be around 10 percent of the strength of your daily dosage.

Dr. Baark of Lufthansa illustrates another use of the "intermediate" injection on a long flight westbound from Frankfurt, Germany, to Los Angeles. Assuming a 1 P.M. departure from Frankfurt, the diabetic accustomed to one injection in the morning and one in the evening would reach the time for his evening shot about five hours after takeoff—about three hours before arriving, say, in New York for a short stopover. At that point, five hours after the flight took off, he would retire to the lavatory and administer his evening injection. If his final destination was Los Angeles, he would still have nine more hours in the air ahead of him before arriving at 8 P.M. That's the time he would normally take his morning dosage. Presumably, though, he's going to check into his hotel and try to get some sleep. Since he's not going to be physically active, says Dr. Baark, he should take a small intermediate injection and eat a light meal before going to bed. The next morning (by Los Angeles time), he should take his usual dosage—and stick to his habitual schedule from then on.

Eastbound: More often than not, it's an eastbound flight that causes complications for a diabetic on insulin. Unless he plans carefully traveling to Europe, he's liable to have to depart at night, after he's already eaten dinner. About an hour after takeoff, the flight attendants will be offering him another meal. He'll land in Europe, say, at 10 A.M.—4 A.M. back home. The problem is, since insulin dosages and mealtimes are linked, in order to keep his diet and shots in sync, he might run the risk of having his insulin dosages overlap. To prevent this, the British Diabetic Association recommends that if you are flying across four or more time zones eastbound (subtracting four or more hours from your day), you should:

1. Cut your dosage by about 20 percent, if you usually take one shot of "intermediate"-type insulin each day.
2. Cut your second dosage by 20 percent, if you customarily take regular-type insulin (or a blend of regular and intermediate) in the morning and evening.

Some authorities on diabetes suggest, instead of reducing the dosage by a flat 20 percent, that diabetic travelers reduce it in proportion to the percentage of day lost. Flying from New York to London, for instance, means a loss of six hours; six hours is 25 percent of our twenty-four-hour day. Thus, the diabetic would cut his daily dosage by a quarter. Others argue that diabetics who need less than 20 units of insulin daily may not have to cut their dosages at all. In order to find out what's right for you, *you must ask your doctor.*

However, all the medical authorities agree that, before flying, diabetics should observe the following rules:

- Whether you take insulin injections or tablets (which lower your blood sugar and are less of a problem to travelers), get your blood and urine checked shortly before you depart.
- Wear a bracelet that identifies you as a diabetic.
- Check the weather ahead at every city you're planning to visit (your airline reservations agent can often do that for you; some newspapers, such as the *New York Times*, also list the previous day's weather at important cities around the world). As a diabetic, you have to take special precautions to protect yourself against cold weather.
- Carry a brief résumé of your medical history with you and not just in case you require treatment along the way. That Spanish customs official, at the airport in Madrid, may get surly when he sees a syringe in your luggage. In Spain, and in many other countries abroad, at the first suspicion that you're a narcotics user, you are liable to wind up in some dingy dungeon. First they quarantine you—then, much later, maybe they'll ask questions.
- Make sure you carry your equipment—all of it—on board the plane. Anyone who travels by jet long enough eventually gets his luggage temporarily misplaced. Having the best equipment in the world won't do you much good if you're in Denmark—and your luggage is in Dubrovnik.
- Put some sugar cubes or candy in your pocket before you board, in case you need carbohydrates during the flight.
- Be sure to ask your doctor what other items you should add to this list.

ORAL CONTRACEPTIVES

The birth-control pill is one of today's most widely used drugs. Since it has to be taken at a regular time of the day, you may have to adjust your schedule if you intend to fly east or west across several time zones. Exactly how you should reset your internal clock to match your shorter day (eastbound) or longer one (westbound) will depend on whether you are used to taking your pill in the morning or in the evening, and the departure time, direction, and destination of your flight. If given the proper information, your gynecologist should be able to help you make the necessary adjustment.

Whatever schedule he or she works out for you, you should make sure you change over to a pill that is effective for at least thirty-six hours. And you must start taking this pill one month before the beginning of your trip.

To give you an example of the kind of adjustment in your schedule you may have to make, let's suppose that you normally take your pill in the evening and that you are going to fly from New York to Tokyo, via Los Angeles and Hawaii. You would take a pill about four hours after leaving Hawaii, again at noon after you arrive in Tokyo, and then, as you do at home, every evening in Tokyo from then on. On your return flight, you would take your pill on your second airborne day, in the late evening in Los Angeles, and as usual on the third day.

Now that you know how to adjust your medication schedule to the new rhythm imposed on you by jet lag, your preflight preparations are almost complete.

You have chosen a flight that suits you and you have in mind a particular seat. You may have decided to preadapt your body clock by means of a special diet. In any case, you've purchased that picnic basket, planning to fill it with snacks you can substitute for the airplane meals. You know how long it will take you to recover from jet lag at your destination. To make sure nothing happens to your health to slow down that recovery period, your medical kit sits next to your picnic basket, ready to be packed in your carryall and taken into the cabin of the plane. If you require any special medication, you've included that in your kit, too.

Now, finally, your departure day has arrived.

II
On the Plane

9

Departure Day

At any hour of the day or night, there are a million human bodies hurtling through the stratosphere. Diplomats cruising toward crucial summits; corporate executives empowered to seal multimillion-dollar deals; ordinary tourists, splurging their hard-earned cash on a sunny, sexy hideaway in southern France. Surgeons, opera singers, journalists, tennis stars, fashion designers, politicians, actors, artists, talent agents—all eyes staring at three or four movie screens, ears tuned to a ten-track stereo system, palates savoring plates of tasty morsels and tempting alcoholic beverages.

But the commercial carriers' assault on the senses can't conquer jet lag. Hour after hour, passing through each new time zone, internal systems—neural, hormonal, metabolic—grow more restless, mutually out of phase. Body functions slip out of sync with the external world.

How can you avoid, on the airplane, compounding the jet lag effects you are sure to suffer once you reach your destination? What you do in the hours before you board the airplane is crucial.

ATTITUDE

Comedienne Joan Rivers insists that the most pleasant experience she ever had with an airplane flight involved one scheduled from Washington, D.C., to New York. "The plane never took off," said Joan. "We had to drive."

If, like Joan Rivers, you don't wake up with a positive attitude on the morning of your flight, it's going to be rough rowing all day. Your adrenaline pumping, your heart thumping, by the time

63

you board the airplane you'll be a basket case. You'll be so drained, so fatigued when you eventually land, you'll be as easy a victim for jet lag to mug as a tipsy tourist in Times Square. Later, I'll tell you some ways to overcome your fear of flying on board the airplane. For now, this morning of your departure, while you perform your last-minute chores—and there had better be darn few of them!—here are some facts you might want to mull over:

- More people are killed each year by lightning than in air crashes.
- Being an airline pilot is not considered a hazardous occupation; a pilot's life insurance rates are about the same as a bank teller's.
- For every hour your airplane spends in the air, it will spend five hours on the ground being serviced. If you took care of your automobile as carefully as a commercial carrier takes care of its plane, you would need a trio of full-time mechanics, checking virtually every component each time you pulled into your driveway. Every five hundred miles you'd have to put on a new set of tires. Each twenty-five hundred miles, you'd have to give your car a total tuneup. When your odometer reached ten thousand miles, your three full-time mechanics would haul the engine out, take it apart, replace the worn components, then put it together again. At twenty-five thousand miles, no matter what your engine's condition, you would have to get rid of it and install a brand-new one.
- Finally, remember that when it comes to health, more people die immediately before and after a flight—from excitement, last-minute rush, and lugging heavy baggage—than ever die during a flight. Take it easy. Look good, feel good, but stay cool.

DRESSING FOR YOUR FLIGHT

If you are smart, you'll be leaving on a flight that gets you to your destination in time to retire with the natives. Eastbound, that means a morning departure; westbound, by early afternoon at the latest. However, particularly traveling toward the east, some of you may have to depart in the evening or at night. There may not

be an earlier flight, or you may not be able to lose a day of work.
If you are going to depart after work, without stopping off at home
for a quick change of clothes, make sure that that morning you
dress as comfortably as possible. Cabin crews can easily distin-
guish veteran travelers from novices. The veteran, on a long flight,
enters the airplane wearing loose-fitting clothes, of fabrics that
don't require a cleaner's touch if they get tainted with ketchup.
The novice, in contrast, arrives corseted and sharply creased. His
attire is more suitable for a ball at Buckingham Palace than an
airborne subway rush-hour crush. *The rule is: Any discomfort
you endure on the plane will eventually deepen your suffering
from jet lag.*
Therefore:

- Wear loose-fitting clothing that doesn't stain easily—in other
  words, leave the silk blouse packed until you slink, at midnight, into that sexy disco.
- And don't forget something well worn and comfortable for
  your feet. In case you do forget your feet, they may remind
  you of their existence by turning into a pair of dirigibles by
  midflight.

"There's something about the pressurized cabin that makes
my feet swell," said Cynthia Gregory, ranked top among
America's prima ballerinas. "You can't see my ankle bones;
it's all just puff."

The swollen-feet syndrome afflicts all air travelers, she
added, but dancers seem to suffer more, perhaps because their
muscles are so fully developed. Cynthia Gregory fights the
phenomenon by flying first class, choosing, whenever possible, one of the many airlines that offer seats with flip-up
footrests. She particularly recommends the first-class seats
of the Brazilian national airline, Varig. Not long ago, Rio was
one of the stops in her annual four-month dance tour. "When
I walked off that plane," she recalled, "I could have danced
through the aisles of the airport."

Cynthia Gregory did not, of course, dance through the aisles
of Rio's airport. Instead, she went directly to her hotel and
did what she always does after any long jet flight. She asked
room service to send up a couple of champagne buckets filled
with ice. Then she filled each bucket with a dainty foot, too.

Icing down your feet when you arrive is an excellent idea. So is packing a pair of soft slippers.

- Finally, be sure to remember to bring a sweater or light jacket with you into the airplane. Even if you're traveling from someplace torrid to someplace tropical, you may need it; when you get sleepy and your body temperature falls, an airplane cabin can seem awfully chilly. The air pressure inside is equal to five thousand to seven thousand feet above sea level.

SKIN CARE

As you are dressing on the day of your departure, take a look at your face in the mirror. A woman may spend hundreds of dollars a year on skin creams and blusher and all the other paraphernalia of looking pretty. Obviously, she wants to look her best during that trip abroad. So, look in your mirror. Engrave the memory of that smooth, unblemished skin into your mind because, unless you are careful, it may be the last time you are your own work of art until you return.

In an airplane cabin, humidity is only about 2 percent (and we are accustomed to humidity of at least 30 percent here on earth). "That's the same as sitting out in the desert," said Dr. James Crane, the former FAA flight surgeon. "Although you don't realize it, you are continuously sweating."

The low humidity can cause problems if you wear contact lenses; it dries out the fluid normally present on the surface of the eyes. Worse, since looking good is an essential part of feeling good for most people, it can wreak havoc on your skin. The low humidity in an airline cabin is the reason such a large portion of a flight attendant's pay goes for skin moisturizers. For a professional model, the price can be even higher.

"One of my main problems on a plane is that I'm usually coming back from some island, where, no matter what I do, I almost always end up getting black," said superstar model Christie Brinkley, who rocketed to fame, in a bathing suit, from the covers of *Sports Illustrated*. "And that is already so drying for the skin, I try and combat it with every means possible. But when you get on the plane, having that dry, dry air can sometimes make you just start flaking. By the time I get back to work, ready for a new job the next day, I can be totally dried out, flaking, a mess. And I have no more sunshine to blend in the tan again.

"That's why," Christie added, "on a plane, I'm very careful to drink tons of water the entire trip. That helps keep you from becoming dehydrated and flaking. And, of course, I keep applying plenty of skin moisturizers throughout the flight."

CHECKING IN

"I've never had trouble with airport security," said comic Joan Rivers. "I keep begging them," she added, "to strip me for drugs."

The airport security check—though absolutely necessary and ultimately comforting—is only one of several hurdles you have to clear before you can board your flight. Still, many people have a habit of making mad last-minute dashes to the airport. When I was an airline reservations agent, I tried to warn passengers against this tactic. I would point out that the airlines generally advise travelers to check in an hour before an international flight and at least half an hour before a domestic one. I would point out to the passenger that by arriving early, he could avoid the long lines that queue up at both the ticket counter, if you are sending some luggage, and at the boarding gate, if you have used sidewalk check-in service and simply need a boarding pass. I would remind a smoker that if he didn't get to the airport early enough, he might find the smoking section already filled.

However, there was one excellent reason for showing up early that I didn't reveal to the passengers who telephoned. Periodically, our supervisor would monitor our conversations to assess our performance. No one was going to give me a gold star for warning a passenger that he might be "bumped" off his flight.

A friend of mine once worked for the airline that runs the shuttle between New York and Washington, D.C. The idea behind that shuttle is, if one plane gets filled at the time you want to fly, they'll bring up another one so that no one gets left behind. The implication is that a passenger is guaranteed a seat. However, my friend was told never to use that word—*guarantee*—to a passenger. When a passenger asked if he was guaranteed a seat, my friend was told to reply: "We *assure* you a seat." *Assure* and *guarantee* might sound like synonyms to a traveler, but they mean different things to a company lawyer. Suppose, for some reason, the airline simply ran out of shuttle planes at a particular hour, before it ran out of passengers. *Guarantee* was too ironclad, while *assure* was full of legal loopholes.

There were lots of other things we never told passengers—for instance, that there was no penalty for *not* canceling a flight they decided not to take; that their airline ticket was good for an entire year; that if they wanted to fly "standby," there was nothing stopping them from booking, under phony names, half the seats or more on the airplane, assuring (but not guaranteeing) that they'd get one for half-price when they showed up at the airport. And we didn't tell them about "bumping."

On popular routes, at peak travel times, the airlines regularly overbook flights. They argue they have to overbook certain flights because too many passengers either cancel at the last minute or don't bother canceling their reservations at all. That's why, on almost any flight, no matter how booked your travel agent tells you it is, you can usually board as a standby passenger.

However, once in a while—and once is far too often if it spoils your holiday or business trip—every soul who has made a reservation will show up at the airport. You may have made your reservation six months ago, and someone else only that morning. It doesn't matter. Whoever gets into line first gets on first. The money you'll get from the airline if you are bumped will be small compensation and no consolation if it means losing a day of your vacation or that reservation at the hotel of your dreams.

So, keeping from getting bumped off your flight is one good reason to get to the airport early. There are other reasons just as compelling.

STANDBY FARES

Flying standby isn't really recommended if you're trying to avoid the insecurity and last-minute rush that can compound jet lag. However, if you truly feel you are psychologically capable of braving the unknown or if the cost of your trip is more burdensome than the possibility you might miss the plane you want, you might consider risking it. Travelers to many major domestic and international cities can save up to half the fare by going standby.

Off season, as I pointed out before, most airliners take off with plenty of vacant seats. If you are traveling in the off season and don't have to be at your destination at a specific time, try this tactic: A few days before the flight you want is scheduled to depart, telephone the airline and ask the reservations agent about your chances of flying standby. The agent will check, in the computer, how many seats have already been booked on that flight. She may even be able to tell you the exact number of seats left. In any case, ask her if your chances of getting on the plane are good, fair, or poor. If she says "good," you'll probably make that flight.

Call again the day before your flight. If seats are still available, plan to get to the airline ticket office nearest to you (or to the special standby ticket counter at the airport) as early as possible. Especially on many international flights, you don't have to wait until everyone has boarded the plane till you find out if there's room for you, too. As early as 4 A.M., in some cases, at the airport, you can get ticketed. And once you have your standby ticket and your seat assignment, you have no greater chance of getting "bumped" off the flight than a passenger paying full fare.

Once on the flight, you get absolutely the same service as everyone else. The nerves you rubbed raw running around that morning may be salved on board by the knowledge that the passenger sitting next to you paid twice as much for the same privilege of getting motion sickness.

AIRLINE CLUBS

Airports aren't usually ideal places in which to have to wait around. You walk past the sliding door, nervous and anxious and excited, and are immediately accosted by some vacant-eyed zombie, a grinning young girl who has nothing better to do with her time than pin flowers to people's chests. Escaping from her thorny clutches, you are next panhandled by the guy who *must* have your signature on a pro-nuclear-power petition. You check your baggage. You walk to your departure gate and take a seat. What are you going to do for an hour before you board your plane? Sit and stare at your fellow passengers, who, like you, are wondering if the flight will take off on time—and land in one piece?

For a small annual membership fee, you can find a safe haven in plush surroundings. If you travel often enough—and one late-departing international night-flight is enough for me—it may be worth your while to join an airline club. Once upon a time, the Ambassador and Senator Lounge and Sun King Club and their like limited their membership to travelers who logged a minimum of one hundred thousand air miles each year. The courts ended this discriminatory policy. Now, for a yearly fee ranging from twenty-five to forty dollars, you, too, can evade the stressful chaos of a crowded airport terminal. And stress, of course, is what turns a minor case of jet lag into a jumbo-size one.

Here are some of the airline clubs' advantages:

1. The petitioners and flower-pinners can't pursue you into this sanctuary. Since their ultimate themes usually center on either destruction or salvation, you will be spared their reminders of man's fragile mortality—and thus, your own, while hurtling through space in a jet.

2. Going from the momentous to the mundane, airline clubs are usually the only facilities in an airport that stock diet soda. If you are addicted to Tab or any other of the diet drinks, you'll have to pay the airline-club premium if you want to imbibe your low-cal favorite.

3. Ever try to telephone your wife or husband or girl or boy friend from an airport-terminal telephone? It's a little difficult to get intimate when you're being inundated by the chatter of several hundred spectators. Businessmen—who always seem to have to call their secretaries moments before their planes depart—may find the need to shout counterproductive. In contrast, in the airline clubs, the telephone booths are spacious, often separated from one another, sometimes soundproofed—and almost always available.

4. Most airline clubs have agents on the premises who will book your seat on the airplane, so that you don't have to stand in line, and will assist you with any other travel arrangements you want to make.

5. The airline clubs also serve your stomach, offering a variety of snacks, depending on the time of day. If you can't resist the temptation, they also have ways of raising your spirits—with an assortment of distilled ones. But you should pass up the temptation to booze on the ground.

6. Businessmen may want to make use of the conference rooms the airline clubs make available. More and more, busy executives are choosing to interrupt their itineraries for business meetings at an airport. Unwilling to "waste time," these hard-drivers depose executives junior to themselves to schedule an airport conference during the boss's three-quarter-hour layover between connecting flights. You can earn significant Brownie points by bringing your boss into the conference room of a luxurious airline club.

7. If you are a Californian, and thus accustomed to getting a prearranged page during any deal at the Polo Lounge, you can put on the same airs in an airline club. They will take messages for you—and even, at your request, trumpet them loudly across the room: "Frank Sinatra calling Mr. Himmelfarb!"

8. Remember the secret decoder rings you got by mailing in cereal box tops when you were a kid? (I had to wait ten consecutive weekdays once, while an announcer verbally tapped out: "Kids, tell your Moms to buy ————.") When you join an airline club, you get a secret number, too—a special reservations telephone number, which allegedly increases your chances of getting an airline agent to respond so that you can book a flight.

9. Finally, for those of you who won't cross the street unless doing so engenders a tax break from Uncle Sam—your airline-club membership fee is tax deductible.

For some people, though, passing time in an airport terminal is no laughing matter.

THE HANDICAPPED

Disabled travelers not only have to get to the airport earlier than others, but they should make their reservations sooner, too. Some airlines restrict the number of handicapped travelers they will carry on any particular flight.

I've already pointed out the advantages to a disabled person of choosing a wide-body aircraft, specifically a 747 when it's available.. And don't forget to select one of those three seats on the right-hand side of the entry door to the aircraft.

That's not the end of your strategics, however, but the beginning. Despite the airlines' good intentions, many disabled travelers don't exactly feel the commercial carriers cater to their needs.

Itzhak Perlman, the renowned violinist, reviles the airlines for
what he considers their "horrendous treatment" of handicapped
travelers. He insists that airline wheelchairs are often too small,
when they are available at all. On board, he only wishes he fit
into an airline bathroom as easily as his precious Stradivarius fits
into the storage bin over his seat. Maneuvering in an airline lavatory, he said, is "like putting on a suit three sizes too small."

As far as wheelchairs are concerned, they offer the disabled
traveler one big incentive to get to the airport early on the day
he departs. If you don't get a wheelchair early, you might not get
one at all. Even if a wheelchair is available, you won't be able to
use it to mount the airplane. Sometimes an airline doesn't provide
passengers boarding its smaller jets with jetways; you have to
walk down a set of stairs, cross a strip of Tarmac, then climb
some more steps into the airplane cabin. The airline will provide
you with a boarding chair and some bearers, but your best tactic
is to avoid this regal entrance by flying from big-city airports,
where such inconveniences are less likely to occur.

And what about your own wheelchair? Can you take it on board
the plane or do you have to ship it with the rest of your luggage?
And what happens when you arrive, if you did have to send your
wheelchair in the airplane's cargo bay? Will there be a wheelchair
at the end of your flight, so that you can get to the luggage carousel
to collect your own wheelchair? Ask the airlines reservations
agent or your travel agent when you book your flight. And then
get to the airport as early as you can on the day of your departure
so that you can ask the same questions over again—to make sure
you get all the answers you need.

Airplane lavatories, as Itzhak Perlman indicated, present the
disabled traveler with even greater problems. They are difficult
for the disabled passenger to get to (as I noted before, no wheelchair is slim enough to negotiate an airliner aisle, nor would
government safety regulations allow you to use one on board
anyway). And once you do get into the lavatory, it's difficult to
accomplish what you came for.

Some disabled passengers, giving such maneuvers their highest
priority, choose a seat right next to the lavatory. Unless your
physical condition offers no alternative, however, I don't recommend this tactic. Those seats are noisy and sometimes nau-
seating; the aisle beside them is often overcrowded with relief-
seekers.

Other handicapped passengers try modifying their intake of liquids before and during the flight, as a way of keeping their trips to the lavatory to a minimum. The danger is that they run the risk of becoming seriously dehydrated. Such modifications should only be made on the advice of your doctor, who may also offer medications that can help.

In any case, don't try asking the stewardess to help you to perform your private biological functions. They do not, by their own regulations, have to assist immobilized passengers who need to use the toilet—and undoubtedly will refuse to do so if asked.

Your best solution, if using the lavatory has been an awesome obstacle for you on past flights, is to fly with a companion who will assist you if you need help.

For further information, write for the U.S. Department of Transportation's free booklet entitled *Access Travel: Airports.* The address is: Architectural and Transportation Barriers Compliance Board, 330 C Street, S.W., Washington, D.C. 20201.

JETTING WITH YOUNG CHILDREN

Infants under three months apparently do not suffer from jet lag; their biological rhythms haven't set into rigid cycles yet. But that doesn't mean they can't, inadvertently, add to your own case of jet lag when you land. Your child can suffer from the conditions in the airplane cabin, and his or her discomfort will only increase your own. In order to keep any stressful complications from spoiling your trip, the aeromedical and airline specialists advise you to:

- Put everything you need to care for your baby during the flight in a waterproof bag. Make sure your baby's formula is already prepared. A stewardess will warm up the bottle for you.
- Book that seat facing a bulkhead of the plane so that the flight attendant can clip on one of the bassinets she's carrying on board. If you bring your own bassinet onto the plane, you have to pay for the seat (half-fare for an infant) you're going to strap it to.
- Refrain from swaddling your infant in tight-fitting garments, no matter how cute they make him or her look. Your baby's

clothes should be just as loose-fitting and comfortable as your own.

- When it comes time to board the aircraft, the airline agent at the gate will probably ask the elderly and infirm and families with infants to board the plane before everyone else. Don't sit there smoking that last cigarette. You need the time, and that uncrowded aisle, to construct a comfortable environment for you and your child on the plane.

- Leave your baby's car seat at home. The flight attendants won't allow you to strap your infant in it on the plane, since those car seats aren't approved for use during takeoffs and landings. And what will the airline provide you with instead, to protect your child during those potentially dangerous ascents and descents? The answer is . . . absolutely nothing. In fact, the airlines insist that, during takeoff and landing, you hold your baby in your arms—a dictum that a number of organizations concerned with child safety find infuriating. They argue that holding an infant in your arms is certainly no safer in the air than it is in an automobile. If the airplane has to take a sudden evasive maneuver, you may let go of your child inadvertently . . . and send him or her hurtling across the cabin.

  I believe that the Federal Aviation Administration should compel the airlines to devise—and supply to any traveler who needs it on board—an infant seat equivalent to the one parents put in their cars. Until that day arrives, however, the only way to protect the most vulnerable member of your family is to squeeze him or her between your body and your own safety belt. Your infant may be uncomfortable for the few minutes it takes to reach cruising altitude, or to land on the airport runway, but at least you'll know he or she will be safe in the event of an emergency.

- Keeping your infant tied down with your own safety belt on takeoff or landing can get complicated, however. Especially during the descent, the change in cabin pressure may give your child an earache. If your infant does start crying, give him or her the bottle. Sucking on the nipple will help your baby clear his or her ears.

10

The Fear of Flying

As soon as you board the plane and locate your seat, ask a flight attendant for a pillow and a blanket. According to the experts, the pillow provides the psychological security of a familiar sleeping environment; the blanket helps retain body heat when your temperature drops during sleep.

Some passengers, of course, won't be comforted at all. Nothing can increase jet lag when you land as much as stress during your flight. And there is no surer or more devastating catalyst of stress on board an airplane than the very fear of flying itself.

THE FEAR OF FLYING

For years, John Madden was the head coach of the Oakland Raiders football team, known for both his winning teams and his Academy Award caliber theatrics on the sidelines. When a referee's call infuriated him, he would gesticulate like a raging Roman— a bear of a man, prowling from one end zone to the other, in search of an elusive Super Bowl ring that finally, after Super Bowl XV, fell into his grasp.

Season after season, Madden led his men on marathon gypsy caravans across the skies. Throughout his life, he had never enjoyed flying, but he had learned to accept it. Flying was a part of the territory; no more risky than quarterback Jim Plunkett fooling the defense with a deep pass on third-down-and-inches; as natural as Madden's own ascension into the CBS broadcast booth after he decided his coaching career had ended.

Not long after Madden started broadcasting pro football for CBS, he was jetting home to California following a game in Milwaukee. "It was a perfect flight," he recalled later. "Smooth. A nice day.

No problems. And I started getting this feeling of panic, weakness—you know, where your legs go weak and your palms sweat. I couldn't sit down," Madden added. "I just kept pacing."

Madden went to see a doctor, who found him in perfect physical health. So he flew again—and again experienced that panic. He broadcast another game for CBS, this time in Tampa, then flew to Houston to catch a connecting flight home.

"I sat down and I felt fine," he said. "Then the stewardess closed the door and that feeling came over me. I felt like I had to get out. It had nothing to do with the height or the flying, because we weren't even rolling yet. It was claustrophobia. With the Raiders, we flew charter and I always knew that I had some control. But here, on a commercial flight, I had no control. So, there was panic. I thought, 'Well, it will go away in a minute.' It didn't. I was just miserable all the way to Houston, and when I landed, I said to myself, 'I don't need this.' So I got off and went to a hotel and took a train back home the next day. And," he added, "I haven't been on an airplane since."

Few passengers experience symptoms so distressing as those that afflicted John Madden. But even those of us least susceptible to panic on board an airplane understand the feeling behind his phobia. Some say that flying in a commercial airliner may be the ultimate act of faith: You deliver your body and soul into the hands of someone you don't know; you can't even see where you are going. If the bus breaks down, you flatter yourself that you can drive it. But if the plane "breaks down"? Even if you are a private pilot, the technological maze in the commercial pilot's cockpit will mystify you. In fact, I have found that a few of my friends who are private pilots are among the most fearful fliers—in a commercial plane—of all.

Adding to the uncertainty are those unnerving thumps and groans—the sound of an airliner's muscle as it flexes to fly into space. The more you can transform this noise into music—understanding the sensations of an airplane in normal operation—the less stress you'll experience.

THE SIGHTS AND THE SOUNDS

1. Everyone has boarded the airplane. You are in your seat, waiting for the airport tractors to pull the plane back so that it

can taxi to the runway under its own power. Suddenly, an alarm starts ringing. Should you start climbing over your neighbors toward the emergency exits? Probably not. When the jetway you used to enter the plane is being withdrawn, an alarm sounds, telling the flight attendants to lock the airplane door.

2. Next, the predeparture calm of the cabin is shattered by some heavy hammering. Could it be, you think, that you are making too much noise and the tenants in the apartment below are complaining? No, you realize, this is an airplane. Maybe a mechanic is trying to tack on a loose wheel. Maybe you should have taken another flight. . . .

Fear not. The hammering and heaving in the belly of the airliner is your baggage being loaded. Don't worry about that being damaged either. Your suitcases are encapsulated in thick, sturdy containers, which glide into the airplane's cargo bay on rollers.

3. Now you—and only you, unfortunately—notice what seems like smoke wafting out of the air vents near your seat. There may be drops of liquid dripping, too. Doesn't anyone on board realize that the plane is on fire and that there's a leak in the fuel line? Stay cool; staying cool is what the "smoke" and droplets are all about. They are simply vapor and condensation from the air conditioning, common when the cabin air is humid and the system is first turned on.

4. You are taxiing out toward the runway, when suddenly you slow down almost to a halt amidst a dirge of ear-splitting groans and grinding gears. It sounds as if some large—undoubtedly indispensable—part is falling off, impeding your plane's progress as the part scrapes along the ground. In fact, it simply means that the brake pads were recently replaced and aren't yet bedded in.

5. Takeoffs, if you've been wondering, are less dangerous than landings—in terms of the complexity of the maneuvers your pilot has to execute. Does that make you feel better? That heavy thump you just heard as your plane took flight certainly didn't. Don't worry. As the plane lifted off, its main landing gear fell to the full extension (but not off the plane) of its shock-absorbing struts. Or the noise may have been caused by the automatic system designed to brake the wheels before they retract.

6. Your knuckles turn white gripping the arms of your seat: What about that vibration humming through the superstructure? No, the plane is not about to fall apart. The rumbling vibration that occurs occasionally just after takeoff is due to an out-of-

balance tire, spinning free before the gear is retracted. It will not impede a smooth landing at your destination.

Not that a smooth landing is always the most desirable one. On a short runway or in a gusty crosswind, a firm touchdown is far safer than a gentler one. Besides, whether the landing is rough or smooth depends more on luck than the pilot's skill. He is sitting so high off the runway and so far forward of the landing gear that it is nearly impossible for him to always anticipate the instant the tires will collide with concrete.

7. The unnerving noises aren't over yet. As the plane soars into the air, its engines suddenly seem to die and you feel the aircraft turning. Has your pilot lost all power? No way. He is simply undertaking a noise-abatement maneuver, reducing power temporarily to avoid offending the inhabitants of the residential neighborhood below.

8. Then you will hear a terrific thump. That means the landing gear is being locked into the belly of the aircraft. The high-pitched whine you hear is the sound of the hydraulic pump system slowly retracting the flaps and leading edge slats (you can see them on the forward and aft edges of the wings) that made the wings bigger to help the plane take off.

9. The airplane is still climbing toward its cruising altitude. You look out the window and see a stream of fluid "leaking" from somewhere on the wing. It's not the airplane's jet fuel dribbling away. That liquid you see flowing over the top of the wing is just a sheet of vapor, condensing into water in the humid air.

10. Then you hit some turbulence and notice out the window that the airplane's wings are flapping, like a terrified goose struggling to get off the ground. Don't reach for your emergency flotation cushion: The wings of a large aircraft are supposed to flex when the weather on high gets rough. The idea is to make them supple enough to absorb blows caused by opposing upward and downward drafts. The wingtips of a 747, for instance, are made to move through an up-down arc of about ten feet. Incidentally, while a Concorde's wings stay stiff, its entire fuselage may start to flop during takeoff or rough weather at low altitudes. That's normal, too; its superstructure is built to expand and contract at various temperature extremes.

11. About twenty minutes to a half-hour before you are scheduled to land, you'll suddenly hear the engines seem to lose their

power, followed by a bumpy sensation, as if your aircraft is riding over airborne potholes. The engine deceleration is due to your pilot dropping to a lower altitude. He will do so swiftly, rather than descending in a gradual swoop. Jets use less fuel at high altitudes; to save fuel, the airline companies want them to hang high in the air as long as they can. Thus, your aircraft will dive down somewhat precipitously rather than coast to its final landing approach.

And what about that sensation of riding over potholes? That's *not* caused, as many people believe, by your pilot "reversing the engines." It's caused by his activating of the "spoilers"—doorlike panels on top of the wings that open and literally spill some of the lift-giving airflow, aiding the plane in slowing down and descending as rapidly as possible.

12. After the engines slow down to start your descent, you may hear a clunking and roar that sounds as if your final approach may indeed turn out to be your *final* one. It's only the landing-gear cover opening and the wheels extending.

Then, especially if the pilot faces lower-air turbulence, you may hear the engines furiously roar, as if the pilot is trying to compensate after overshooting his landing approach. Wrong again. During rough weather, the pilot normally will push forward those power levers. Jet engines respond less quickly than piston ones; the pilot has to give them a strong kick to get them thrusting.

FLYING PHOBIAS

One American out of every six, say the experts, is afraid to fly. Of those nearly twenty-five million people, however, a small percentage are not only fearful but, like John Madden, utterly phobic. Knowing what the noises of an airplane mean won't dissolve their dread. Reminding them that, according to Lloyd's of London, it's about twenty-five times safer to travel in an airplane than to travel in a car, won't help much either. Nor will the news that, every day in the United States, the airlines' twenty-five hundred planes safely carry an average of six hundred fifty thousand passengers an average of six hundred miles out of four hundred airports.

Some phobics, like Madden, have decided to forego flying completely. Others who do board a trans- or intercontinental flight risk complicating the jet lag they'll experience when they land. Stress is the ladle that stirs up jet lag's symptoms.

Only your doctor should decide whether or not a tranquilizer before or during the flight will help. But since too many of us have developed too deep a dependency on drugs anyway, the phobic flier might want to try instead some techniques that don't require pill-popping. You only have to do what comes naturally: Breathe. You can learn to overcome your anxiety, say the experts, by practicing deep breathing.

1. Begin at home, by selecting a comfortable armchair—one with support for your head. You should be able to place the soles of your shoes squarely on the floor—something that phobic fliers are too tense to do in an airplane.

2. With your legs uncrossed, lean back and relax. Don't clench your fists; don't set your teeth on edge. Relax, and open that invisible safety valve in your head, allowing any anxious thoughts to escape.

3. Take three deep breaths, using your nose or mouth or both. Each time, inhale and hold your breath while you mentally count to three. Then exhale—and rest a moment, allowing the peace you've gained by exhaling your tension to flood over you.

Each time, breathe in more air than you did the time before. Once you've repeated these simple exercises enough so that you have mastered them, close the safety valve in your head and let your mind recall some marvelously peaceful place you've visited. Pretend you are there. Then review an experience you had in the air that frightened you. Finally, preview, while you do your deep breathing, what is frightening you about the trip you are about to embark on.

4. Fantasize that you are already aboard the aircraft; inhale, hold your breath, then exhale deeply. Remember while you do it that everyone is excited; it's not the inevitable excitement you want to exhale but the irrational fear.

Imagine in your mind all the procedures the flight attendants go through before departure and while the plane is taxiing to the runway. Remember that just because a plane has emergency exits, it doesn't mean you're going to use them. If you live in an apartment, you have a fire escape. Wouldn't it be silly if you found that frightening? Go over in your mind all the little things that have disturbed you on past flights. Reviewing them while you are doing your deep-breathing exercises will drain those moments of their clinging fear.

5. Go out of your way to visit airports. Spend an hour or so simply watching plane after plane after plane smoothly taking off. Get some books and read about how airplanes really work. Knowledge is an antidote to fear. Primitive peoples may fall to their knees and raise their hands in supplication to the heavens when they hear thunder. We just reach for our umbrellas.

6. Again, try to depart on a morning flight. Not only will you arrive at the time closest to your normal bedtime, you won't have to spend the entire day worrying about flying.

7. Again, get to the airport early; a last-minute dash will only intensify your anxiety.

8. Once on board, ask a flight attendant if, before the plane begins to taxi, you can look into the airplane's cockpit. Remember, as I said before, that the man at the controls is probably paying no more for his life insurance than is a bank teller. The reason you'll find him so relaxed and affable is because he knows that he's safer in the air than he was while driving his car to the airport.

He has to be good at what he does, too. Pilots periodically have their skills retested. They are required to perform such maneuvers as flying the plane on only two engines. And notice how relaxed the copilot seems. A copilot with some seniority (and in this day of economic uncertainty, the ones without seniority probably aren't working) can often reject any assignment he chooses to. You can be sure that any pilot who has trouble getting a copilot to fly with him will undergo intense scrutiny by his bosses. The fact that *your* copilot didn't reject the assignment is another sign that your pilot is competent and trustworthy.

9. Go back and sit down. Close your eyes and begin your deep-breathing exercises. When the airplane begins to move, listen for its distinctive sounds. Go over in your mind what each one means. In the air, once the No Smoking sign is turned off, stand up, stroll around. Your flight isn't going to be as terrifying as you imagined. It might even turn out to be fun.

11

Sleep

Doug Wilson, a TV producer responsible not only for some of those scintillating sports shows you see on ABC but for some of the stirring musical themes that accompany them, once took a trip to South America in an airplane that also had on board actress Jacqueline Bisset. Midway through the flight, the lights were dimmed. The passengers curled up in their seats, attempting, as best they could, to fall asleep.

But Doug kept his eyes open long enough to see Jacqueline Bisset pick up a small bag and retire to a lavatory. When she returned, Doug said, "She had changed into a nightgown. She raised the arms of the two empty seats beside her and simply stretched out in her nightgown to go to sleep."

Jacqueline Bisset slept soundly. Doug was up all night, wide-eyed and staring.

Few of us can enjoy the luxury of a chartered flight in the company of a crew of professionals who'll at least pretend to ignore anything we do that's out of the ordinary. Still fewer of us are self-possessed enough to simply slip on our night clothes in order to relax as completely as possible. For most travelers, sleeping on a plane—even with the aid of a blanket and a pillow—is difficult or even impossible. Yet frequent travelers are almost unanimous in agreeing that sleep is an indispensable revitalizer.

"I take planes the way most people take buses, and I find that sleep is the key to reducing jet lag," said Robert Tisch, the president of Loews Corporation.

Jim McKay, ABC's "Wide World of Sports" host, offers a tactical reason to try to catch some shut-eye during the flight. "Sleep on the plane," he counseled. "You may not feel rested when you wake up, but it sure makes the time go quickly."

McKay has devised his own personal strategem to seduce himself into dreamland. "When my eyes get too tired to read anymore," he said, "I start watching the movie. Most of them," he added, "put me to sleep within the first ten minutes."

Other travelers find sleep more elusive. Their problems begin with the airplane seat itself.

Once upon a time, incredible as it may seem today, many aircraft had sleeping compartments on board. A passenger making a long flight in 1930, say, could climb aboard and watch the cabin converted into an airborne "Pullman" as darkness fell. Even as late as 1956, the Douglas DC-7 that offered the first regular transatlantic service (the flight took about ten hours) came equipped with "slumberette" reclining seats and bunks. Accommodation has gone downhill from there.

With the advent of jet aircraft, airplanes moved so fast that a fourteen- or fifteen-hour flight became a rarity. Passengers wouldn't need beds in their cabins, the airlines decided. Besides, to pay for the rising cost of jet fuel, the airlines felt they had to pack as many people in each plane as possible. Seats that converted into bunks took up too much space.

And the airlines were also becoming safety-conscious. A wicker garden chair—fashionable in the smoking lounges of imperial flying boats of the 1930s—might be suitable for the dilettantes who dared long flights in those days, but it wasn't safe enough for our government watchdogs. They were quite willing to sacrifice a passenger's comfort to prevent making him a casualty.

Nowadays, the "bed" you're likely to find aboard your aircraft is only about thirty-four inches front to back, if you are traveling first class, or thirty-two inches in coach class. Measured from the front of one seat to the same point on the one behind it, this distance is called the "pitch" of the seat. If you are traveling on a charter flight, the pitch of your seat may be only a meager twenty-nine inches.

Your seat has many positive qualities. It can withstand an acceleration speed nine times that of gravity forward, and one-and-a-half to four-and-a-half times gravity rearward, sideways, up, and down. It should be noted that your seat could, if the airlines so deemed, be even a lot safer than it already is. If you ever have flown in a military aircraft, you'll have noticed one startling difference from a commercial one. The seats face backward toward the tail of the plane. Seats that face backward are safer because, during a sudden deceleration, the passengers are *supported* by the backrest, instead of being thrown against the seat in front. Why won't the commercial airlines face their seats backward? They are convinced that you would rather "see" where you are going than where you have been.

Nonetheless, not only does your seat provide excellent protection during a sudden stop, but it is designed to provide the best average platform for you to sit, read, eat, or watch a movie. But it is not, by any stretch of the imagination, an adequate bed. Nor is a noisy airplane cabin anything like your bedroom. Counting sheep won't do you much good in an airplane cabin.

"The only thing you can count on," said Jim Arey of Pan American's public-relations department, "is that once you manage to fall asleep, the captain will announce that on your left you can catch a spectacular view of Akron, Ohio."

It's not just the activity in the cabin that keeps you awake. Sleep researchers have shown that almost everyone asleep on a bed will alter positions regularly during the night. By changing your position you force changes in your blood flow, helping to pump stale blood through your heart at regular intervals so that it can be purified. Unfortunately, an airplane seat is far more confining than any bed. Tossing and turning may result in a slipped disk or painful contusions from contact with your neighbor's knobby knee.

And even if the cabin interior mimicked the quiet and calm of your bedroom at home and the bed were a real one, it is unlikely that you would sleep any way but fitfully. Your home mattress— or bed of nails, for that matter—is imbued with special physical and psychological values. It conforms, through usage, to the curves of your body; it offers a familiar, friendly environment. Even a nomad carries his tent and sleeping rug with him.

So, you may be expecting too much if you anticipate sleeping soundly all the way to Paris. Especially if you are in your forties or early fifties, even if you do drowse, you probably won't drift deep enough to enter the REM (rapid eye movement) phase of sleep that scientists insist is so vital to feeling refreshed when you wake up. However, you may be able to pass the time away— and feel better than you otherwise would—if you can take a series of light naps. You may not get deep sleep, but you will be relaxed.

How do you manage even a catnap in the crowded conditions of a jet airplane's cabin? Begin by converting your seat into as close a facsimile of a bed as possible. If the seat (or pair of seats, depending on the type of airplane) beside you is empty, you can lift up its arms, put your pillow under your head and your blanket over you, and curl up in fetal position. Problem solved.

The problem is, of course, that you are unlikely to be lucky enough to have an empty seat or two beside you. Then you'll have to recline your seat, making as much of a hammock out of it as possible. Slide down and stick your feet under the chair in front of you as far as they will go. If you have luggage stored there, place it in an overhead storage bin.

Slippers

There are some items that might help you relax enough to nap. Travelers flying first class always used to find pairs of disposable slippers tucked into the pocket behind the seat in front of them. Airline economies have ended this practice on many flights. Thus, you'll be wise to include a pair of soft slippers in the bag you carry on board, for two reasons: First, the slippers will keep your feet warm, an advantage in the cool airplane cabin; and second, you can use them as substitutes for your shoes, moving about the cabin without offending more conservative passengers for whom the sight of a naked foot or the odor of a sweaty sock might be too much to bear. In any case, remember, you should take off your shoes; your feet might swell during the flight.

Eye Masks

On some flights in first class, you may be offered an eye mask, too. Unfortunately, for some travelers an eye mask is more of a problem than a panacea. If you are accustomed to wearing one at home to keep out the light at night (and I personally do not know anyone who does), then by all means use the one you get free from the airline or bring your own. However, if you don't usually go to sleep wearing an eye mask, you may find it simply makes sleeping on the plane more difficult. My advice is: Try one if the flight attendant offers you an eye mask. If it doesn't help, put it away.

Music

Almost all trans- or intercontinental airlines (except the chartered sardine-can variety) come equipped with multitrack stereo systems. For a three-dollar fee, you can rent a set of headphones, which allow you to hear not only the movie soundtrack but channels featuring comedy albums or interviews or Mantovani or Mozart or Motown or The Who. Will the music help you to get to sleep on the plane?

My seventeen-year-old son cannot fall asleep at night without a rock 'n' roll lullaby pounding through his ears. In contrast, the faintest echo of some combo playing the softest, sweetest music imaginable will keep me wide awake all night. My son and I have reached a compromise: He sleeps wearing light headphones—like the ones used on airplanes. So when he travels to Europe, say, he finds that listening to the rock channel on the airline stereo helps him to sleep. I do not even rent a set of headphones.

If listening to music under headphones (or even without them) is part of your normal sleeping pattern, then that activity is likely to help you nap on a plane. You may, if you own one, consider bringing a high-quality stereo Walkman on board, plus a supply of your favorite tapes; I know businessmen who use them during flights to review crucial conferences they've recorded. These tiny tape players in no way interfere with the operation of the plane.

If music is not a part of your regular pattern, don't expect that airborne sonata to lull you into a coma. The headphones may be more of an annoyance than a soporific. If you find the noise of the aircraft cabin too stressful, try bringing a pair of earplugs along instead.

The fact is, try as they may, some travelers simply find it impossible to nap on a plane. I am one of them. At some unconscious level, I am probably too nervous to sleep, prepared at any moment to start pedaling in case the pilot needs help keeping his craft in the air. Recently, though, I discovered a substitute for sleep that left me, at the end of my flight, more refreshed than ever before. The tip I tried came from the world-renowned writer James Michener.

"I have never fallen asleep on a plane, no matter how exhausted," said Michener, who circles the world giving lectures and collecting material for his books. "My wife sleeps easily, almost immediately, and is thirteen years younger. Yet when the trip is over," Michener added, "she is more exhausted and it takes her quite a few days longer to recover."

Michener's secret is an ability to turn himself off: "To go into hibernation, as it were. I once flew without interruption from London to Tokyo and simply sat in my seat the whole time— with breaks to exercise the legs—and ignored the plane, the passengers, and the passage of time. I arrived in fairly good condition."

However, for those travelers who either can sleep on board an aircraft or who refuse to give up trying to, here is a checklist of dos and don'ts:

Do

- Get a pillow and a blanket as soon as you board the plane.
- Convert the seat or seats next to you, if they are vacant, into a cot by lifting up the armrests.
- Recline your seat back all the way to the rear if the seat or seats next to you are occupied; and spread out.
- Carry a pair of soft slippers on board.
- Remove your shoes and loosen your clothing.
- Remove your carry-on luggage from under the seat in front of you and put it in the overhead storage bin.

Don't

- Try to fall asleep listening to the music on your in-flight stereo unless a musical lullaby is part of your regular sleeping pattern.
- Wear an eye mask unless you are used to sleeping with one at home.
- Take tranquilizers unless your family doctor gives you the okay to do so.
- Worry if you don't get to sleep; the sleep you do get on a plane probably isn't all that beneficial anyway. Jet lag makes sure of that. The idea is—relax.

SMOKING

For some people, the notion of relaxing without a cigarette dangling from their lips is a ridiculous one.

If you are an inveterate chain smoker, as I am, you have already grown such a thick skin to arguments against the habit that nothing I can say is likely to have the slightest influence over your decision to puff away throughout your plane ride. Like you, I have seen the photographs of lungs tinted black by too much tobacco. I have been inundated by all those antitobacco ads on television. (Whenever I see one, I get so nervous I have to immediately light up another cigarette.) I have heard, like you, the heavy footsteps behind me of cancer, heart trouble, emphysema, and a hundred other dreaded diseases. Obviously, nothing I've encountered was terrifying enough to turn me off tobacco.

However, I no longer smoke when I am traveling in an airplane, unless I am flying with a companion who insists on sitting in the smoking section. Why? I simply cannot tolerate the cattle-car conditions back there. Crowded into the tail section of the airplane, their bodies wracked with coughs, their gaping mouths gasping at the unclean air, smokers on board an aircraft get a preview of their habit's terminal hell. The fact is that the effects of smoking aboard an airplane may be even worse than smoking on the ground.

In an earlier era of flying, the biggest problem passengers faced was the possibility of monoxide poisoning from engine exhaust that seeped into the cabin. Jet engines and pressurized cabins eliminated that danger. Nowadays, the only lethal gas you have to worry about is cigarette smoke. At a high altitude—and remember, inside the airplane cabin, you may be halfway up the slope of a towering fourteen-thousand-foot mountain—cigarette smoke can actually inactivate the hemoglobin in your blood, enough to induce in you a temporary anemia. In fact, a chronic smoker will feel as if he is flying at twice the altitude of most pressurized cabins.

Why does smoking affect you even more in the air than it does on the ground? To begin with, the humidity in the airplane cabin may be only 2 percent, versus a minimum of about 30 percent on the ground, because the airplane's air conditioners are constantly sucking out almost every bit of moisture. Furthermore, there's less oxygen in the cabin's air. These two factors combine to increase the quantity of carbon monoxide that a smoker absorbs into his bloodstream. And this increment of carbon monoxide reduces slightly the amount of oxygen your blood can carry. As a result, your heart has to work a little harder. You become more fatigued. And the more fatigued you are, the more your body clock gets gummed up.

So don't smoke on the plane if you can help it. You'll be helping not only yourself but your loved ones and fellow travelers, too. At almost zero humidity, smoking in an airplane is highly irritating to the eyes and nose and throat linings—not only yours but everyone else's, too. Choose a seat at least four rows in front of the smoking section; you can always walk back, sit down, and puff away, returning to your own seat when you are through.

If you must smoke, select a seat in the first row of the smoking section so that no smoke will be blown back into your face by the air conditioners.

DRINKING

"I don't drink, so I cannot comment on the effects of alcohol," said author James Michener. "Yet some of the happiest travelers I have ever seen have been completely stoned within a half-hour of takeoff. What the effects were the next day," Michener added, "I wouldn't like to guess."

We've all seen them in the air: tipsy tourists, stumbling down the airplane aisle or cackling hilariously in their seats, having one helluva good time while you and I nervously await an end to our airborne ordeal. People who drink too much on an airplane act happy, all right—a lot happier because they are a lot drunker than they ever intended to be. And when they land, unfortunately, their boisterous humor will be damped by a suitcaseful of side effects. Air travel turns an average hangover into a haymaker.

Alcohol and Altitude Don't Mix

According to Ross A. McFarland, professor of aerospace health and safety at the Harvard School of Public Health, the effects of alcohol and altitude are additive. Dr. McFarland and other investigators have convincingly proved, in experiments undertaken at different altitudes, that because of the decreased atmospheric pressure, the farther above sea level you are, the faster alcohol will reach your blood and the higher the alcohol levels in your blood will be. In a jet aircraft, cruising along at about thirty-five thousand feet, the cabin atmosphere pressure is equivalent to an outside altitude of about five thousand to seven thousand feet above sea level. Alcohol at that altitude is approximately 33 percent more potent than in your local earthbound saloon.

In other words, three dry martinis in the air are as lethal as four (some scientists say as many as five) on the ground. And in-flight hangovers are probably at least a third worse than normal ones. Like cigarette smoke, alcohol poisons the tissue cells, preventing them from utilizing oxygen properly. The reduced oxygen in the plane, plus the lowered level in your blood, may implant the late swing-drummer Gene Krupa in your head, beating out on your brain his interminable "Sing Sing Sing" solo.

Yet despite the unpleasant effects of drinking alcoholic beverages during a flight, studies show that most travelers tend to imbibe far more freely than is their custom on the ground. Drinks in the air are inexpensive—on some first-class and red-eye flights they are free. Furthermore, you don't even have to get up out of your seat to obtain one. The flight attendants bring the booze to you.

But the most powerful incentive is that flying actually increases your thirst. Scientists say that the sensation of thirst on board is intensified by a shift of fluids within your body tissue, resulting from the lower atmospheric pressure in the airplane cabin, the fact that you sit for long periods without moving, and the decreased humidity. This lack of moisture in the airplane leads to a drying out of the mucous membranes of your lips, mouth, and throat, adding to your thirst.

Remember:

- Assume that two drinks on the plane are *at least* as potent as three on the ground.
- To minimize the unpleasant side effects, if you must drink, choose wine or beer, spacing your drinks as far apart as possible and alternating your wine or beer with nonalcoholic beverages.
- Again, if you must drink, do so (sparingly) on a westbound flight, not an eastbound one, since alcohol slows the free-running clock. Westbound, you'll be able to justify your alcoholic beverage as an antidote to jet lag.

- Don't drink any alcohol if you are taking any kind of medication. In a jet cabin, mixing alcohol and drugs increases the power of *both*.
- The best advice of all is ... don't drink alcoholic beverages at all in the air, although this is definitely one piece of aeromedical counseling that many jet-setters insist on ignoring. Some, like CBS's Harry Reasoner, argue that the psychological benefits of airborne boozing far outweigh the physical liabilities you'll suffer. "I don't pass up the cocktails," said Reasoner. "If there is ever a time I need them, it's when I'm a mile high in an airplane."

NONALCOHOLIC BEVERAGES

You shouldn't drink alcoholic beverages during a long jet flight. But that doesn't mean you shouldn't drink. The low humidity in the airplane cabin and the lack of moisture in your body tissue lead to dehydration—not a severe case but enough to make you feel fatigued and irritable and thirsty.

Passengers do replenish their fluid deficits, says Dr. F. S. Preston, deputy director of medical services of British Airways. The problem is that they tend to drink the wrong replenishing fluids. Apart from the alcoholic ones, which beverages should you avoid and which should you wolf down to prevent dehydration?

Soft Drinks: Pass up soft drinks during the flight. The carbonation—the gas—in them can give you a stomach ache. At thirty-five thousand feet, because of the decreased atmospheric pressure in the airplane cabin, gases in the stomach and intestines are already 20 percent greater in volume. Soft drinks will only worsen the distension.

Coffee and Tea: Unless you need lots of exercise (or are following a preadaptive diet) and can't think of a better way to get it, embargo these brews, too. Coffee and tea are both mild diuretics; in other words, they speed up the loss of liquid through your kidneys. If you drink them, you'll get all the exercise you need, and more than you probably bargained for, trotting back and forth between your seat and the toilet.

Fruit Juices: Highly recommended. They put water back into your body and contain valuable vitamins. No known negative side effects.

Water: Also highly recommended. Dr. Preston advises his British Airways crew members to imbibe between four and five pints of this elixir whenever they are going to fly, in order to prevent dehydration.

Here's a checklist of tips to help you stay relaxed, without the discomforts of dehydration, during your flight:

- To combat dryness, drink at least eight ounces of fruit juices or water or a combination of both during your flight.
- Eat sparingly on board and avoid alcoholic beverages, which, aside from all their other disruptive side effects, also act to enhance your appetite.
- However, do eat something. "To overeat is not good," said Concorde pilot Captain Michel Butel, "but not to eat at all is also harmful." What other advice would you expect from a Frenchman?

12

Exercise

Comedienne Joan Rivers spends many days each year jetting from her home in Los Angeles to engagements across the country. Too many days to suit Joan Rivers. She doesn't get much pleasure from being cooped up in an airplane cabin. She never has the urge to gaze out the window at the panorama of sky and terrain below. Eating anything that a flight attendant sets in front of her, she is an easy victim for jet lag. And she isn't enamored of others who get too athletic defending themselves from that malaise. "As for people who lift their feet over their heads to relax," said Rivers, "I say, keep your filthy socks to your own area!"

No one recommends that you dangle your dirty stockings over anyone else's head. However, doctors do suggest that you do something during your flight aside from vegetating in your seat. When you aren't sleeping or trying to, how can you pass the time? Not by drinking, not by smoking, not by watching the movie, but by . . . exercising.

However lethargic you are in your daily life, your body is in constant motion. Sitting in a swivel chair in your office, you wiggle, waggle your finger at your secretary; you go to the water fountain; you walk to your car or the bus or subway. . . . Even when you are sleeping, at least once every half-hour you shift the position of your body.

What happens, then, if you suddenly become immobile on a long-distance jet flight? More rapidly than you might imagine, your muscles weaken, your bones shed minerals, your joints stiffen, and your circulation turns sluggish. These physiological effects translate into a host of symptoms that will definitely increase the impact of jet lag. You begin to feel tense, fatigued; your feet swell, you get cramps, and your back aches. If you are traveling with a companion, you may soon become another kind of pain in another part of the anatomy.

Exercise is the answer. But how can you exercise in the constricting confines of an airplane seat? Travel editor Richard Joseph recalled, in a 1973 *Esquire* column, the memory of a lavender-haired matron sitting in the back of a darkened plane, who, he presumed, had been unnerved by all the antiskyjacking checks the passengers had endured before the plane departed. In midflight, the lady pressed her call button. "That man," she told a flight attendant, thrusting an accusing finger at someone a few rows in front of her, "is doing something funny to the roof of the airplane."

"She was right," wrote Joseph. "I was standing on my toes, pushing hard against the ceiling, which I could just reach with my fingertips. It's the best technique I know to reconcile a cranky back to the long hours of sitting in an airplane seat."

The jet-setters, it seems, are learning to fight back against their circadian nemesis. Alaska senator Ted Stevens, the Senate's self-proclaimed champion air traveler, made the sixty-nine-hundred-mile round trip between his home state and Washington, D.C., sixteen times in 1971, his busiest year. Stevens attributed his ability to remain alert and stay healthy during those grueling eighteen-hour round trips to the program of isometric exercises he practiced religiously during every flight.

For Christie Brinkley, the star fashion model, the weak muscles and general physical deterioration caused by long flights are a far more serious problem. Sitting too long on a plane can actually interfere with her career. "My image as a model is mainly a sportive, athletic one," she said. "In every photo, I'm going to be leaping, running, jumping . . . trying to be like a Baryshnikov."

To keep her muscle tone firm enough so that she can leap onto the covers of national magazines, Christie makes sure she exercises regularly—before, during, and after each flight. Your blood vessels may not be imbedded in such a glamorous body, but they still need the same care and coddling if they are going to continue pumping, in defiance of gravity, that vital liquid to your heart.

The commercial airline companies themselves offer tips on how to stay in shape. Although medically advisable, some of these exercise hints are, practically speaking, impossible, given the crowded conditions in today's aircraft. As *Esquire*'s Richard

Joseph pointed out, when one of the airline exercise guides tells you that "You can make up for the confines of the airlines seat by getting up and moving around . . . ," that advice makes very little sense to a passenger packed into the window seat of an economy-class section. "Try it more than once," Joseph added, "and your seatmates will reward you with dirty looks at best. Not to mention the stewardesses trying to push their food and their booze-vending carts up and down the aisles." Of course, no reader of this book will be caught in a window seat in the first place.

A different airline offers its passengers some advice that only a bone surgeon, searching for patients with fractures, could love. Its booklet suggests that travelers counter their fatigue by performing "a few calisthenics in the privacy of the lavatory." Richard Joseph reminded us that, "Anyone who has ever squeezed into an airplane 'rest room' knows it's barely large enough for you to perform the functions for which it was intended. But if you're in the economy class of a crowded 747," he added, "your body will get all the respite from sitting it needs by the simple act of standing in the interminable lines trailing their way through the aisles to the john."

Nevertheless, doing some sort of exercise on the plane—even if it's only periodically strolling around the aisles (there is usually a time, after the meal and the movie, when the cabin turns calm—is not only possible but probably indispensable to warding off the worst effects of jet lag. The exercise you choose may be a simple one—simply stretching your arm out to adjust the air flow of the overhead blower does your circulation good. It may also be a startling one: Reporter Morley Safer of "60 Minutes" says he relieves the back pain he suffers from being squeezed into his seat on a long flight by lying down and stretching out for a moment in the aisle of the airplane cabin. Other jet-setters regularly practice more scientifically regulated sets of exercises. Particularly popular is a program developed by the Scandinavian Airline, SAS.

Several years ago, SAS produced a booklet called *Exercise in the Chair*, containing two separate and supplementary exercise programs. The booklet was in such demand that SAS medical adviser Dr. Folke Mossfeldt (who had helped to originate the system of in-chair exercises) published an enlarged version called *The SAS In-the-Chair Exercise Book*, coauthored by Mary Susan

Miller. Here, reproduced with SAS's permission, are the pair of programs contained in that original pamphlet distributed free to passengers. All of these exercises should be performed while sitting in your seat.

EXERCISE PROGRAM NO. 1

1. *Jogging on the spot.* A warming-up exercise: It makes sense to warm up properly before strenuous exercise. Use simple, rhythmic movements, engaging as many muscle groups as possible. "Jog on the spot" by raising your heels alternately as high as possible. At the same time, raise your arms in a bent position and rock rhythmically forward and back as when walking. Continue one to three minutes.

2. *Rising on the toes.* Improves blood circulation to the legs: Sit with elbows on knees, bending forward with your whole weight pressed down on the knees. Lift up on toes with heels as high as possible. Drop heels and lift toes. Repeat whole exercise thirty times.

3. *Shoulder rolling.* Stimulates the joints, relaxes the shoulder muscles: Joints thrive on regular motion. Smooth, rhythmic movements "lubricate" the inner joint. Move the shoulders gently and rhythmically, at intervals, describing large circles in both forward and backward directions.

4. *Head turning and nodding.* Stimulates joint capsules and cartilage in upper spinal column: It is important to regularly activate the joints to the full extent to the right. Nod a few times. Do the same toward the left. Repeat the entire exercise six times.

5. *Forward bends with stomach in.* Stimulates bowels and blood circulation: Stimulate blood circulation and improve the digestion with this exercise: Draw the stomach in fully. Drop the trunk forward while lifting the front of the feet high up. Place the toes back on the floor, relax the stomach muscles, and raise the body upright again. Repeat some thirty times.

6. *Hand turning.* Stimulates the wrists: The cartilages and joint capsules in the wrists also need stimulation. A good way to achieve this is to turn the hands all the way over and spread the fingers. Return hands to original position and relax them. Repeat fifteen times.

7. *Foot rolling.* Stimulates the ankles: Exercising the ankle joints now and again by rolling the feet in large circles to the full extent of their movement is a valuable form of stimulation. Repeat fifteen times in each direction.

8. *Knees up against the elbows.* Speed up blood circulation: Now and then, preferably at regular intervals, one should increase the blood circulation by setting to work large groups of muscles. This is one way: Drive the left and right knees alternatively up toward the opposite elbow. Fifteen times in each direction.

EXERCISE PROGRAM NO. 2

1. *Rowing while seated.* A warming-up exercise: This warm-up session takes the form of an imaginary "rowing" action. Stretch the arms forward while bending the upper body forward for a rowing "stroke." Lift the forward part of the feet right up, then press down the toes, draw in the arms, and at the same time move the body backward, completing the "stroke." Repeat the exercise for one to three minutes.

2. *Alternate knee raising.* Speeds blood circulation: In this exercise we speed up the blood circulation and flow by lifting the left, right, and finally both legs in succession. Grasp the hands together and "pull." Repeat the exercise ten times each for left, right, and both legs.

3. *"Apple-picking."* Stimulates the shoulders: The shoulder muscles and joints are stimulated by alternately and rhythmically stretching up the arms as if picking fruit from a tree. This exercise is alternated with a rhythmic movement of the shoulders forward and back, holding them in a dropped, relaxed position. Repeat exercise ten times with each arm and the shoulders.

4. *Alternate head turning.* Stimulates joint capsules and cartilage in upper spinal column: Bend the head forward (chin against the throat). Keep the chin against the throat and "bend" the head backward. Turn the head as far as you can to the right and nod three times. Return the head to the front. Do the same toward the left. Repeat the whole exercise ten times.

5. *Rising and sitting.* Improves flow of blood to legs and blood circulation: Speed up circulation and stimulate the passage of blood to the legs with this exercise. Gently rise upward or attempt

to rise, with or without the help of the hands. Sit down again and lift the toes. Repeat exercise thirty times.

6. *Double arm swings.* Stimulates the shoulders: To stimulate the muscles and joints of the shoulders and elbows: Sit with the hands clasped. Swing the arms gently, rhythmically upward and backward, stretching them while turning the palms upward. Bring the arms down again and relax. Repeat the exercise ten to twenty times.

7. *Slalom while seated.* Stimulates the blood circulation: "Slalom-skiing" improves the passage of blood to the legs and stimulates blood circulation. Sit with the heels as far out to the right as possible, with both the hands on the same side. Lift the heels right up and swing them all the way over to the left, while swinging the arms over in the same direction. Repeat the exercise thirty times.

8. *Relaxation, muscle control.* We often tense various muscles unnecessarily for short or long periods, sometimes without realizing it. Training in muscle control and relaxation technique helps counteract this and is beneficial in other ways. Try this exercise: Sit fully relaxed. Breathe evenly and gently, using so-called diaphragm breathing. This involves "filling" the stomach when breathing in, which is an active motion. On breathing out, which is a motion, the air is slowly released and the body sinks into complete relaxation.

In order to become aware of the difference between tensed and relaxed muscles, helping to avoid unnecessary tensing, as mentioned above, practice alternately tensing and relaxing various muscle groups. Repeat the exercise until you feel heavy, pleasantly relaxed.

These SAS exercise programs are designed to keep your muscles toned, your joints flexible, and your blood pumping while you are in the plane. Lufthansa German Airlines supplements these routines by offering a series of isometric exercises, "Fitness in the Chair," helping you to combat your jet lag symptoms once you arrive at your destination. (Some of them can be performed on the plane as well.) All of them take no more than moments to accomplish. None of them requires more "equipment" than you'll find in the most Spartan hotel room. All you need is a flight of stairs, a chair, a wall—and a tennis ball and towel.

"KEEP-FIT TIPS"

Here are Lufthansa's "Fitness in the Chair" exercises, numbers one through ten. If you practice them, you'll find yourself adding a tough veneer of armor, helpful in the defense against jet lag's onslaught:

Keep-Fit Tip No. 1: Muscle-Tone Training

Tighten up a muscle or muscle group with about one-third of your maximum strength. Repeat six times. Exercise rhythmically.

Use systematically for those parts of the body particularly affected by long sitting: thigh (left, right), buttocks (left side, right side), back, and shoulders.

Muscle-tone training is invisible—so it can be performed anywhere, anytime.

Keep-Fit Tip No. 2: Stair Climbing

Every staircase gives you a little fitness training. So pass up every elevator, every escalator.

Stair climbing particularly exercises leg, stomach, and buttocks muscles. It contributes to flexibility of foot, knee, and hip joints.

In a test conducted at the Bayer plant, cardiovascular efficiency improved by an average 26 percent with regular stair climbing (twenty-five stories per day).

Keep-Fit Tip No. 3: Hot Seat

Never sit on a chair too long. Stand up frequently: take a few steps to and fro; work standing up whenever you can.

Another exercise: Get up out of chair, using only one leg (first lift other foot slightly off floor). Right, left, right, left. And so on. Keeps the leg muscles in shape.

Keep-Fit Tip No. 4: Dictate in Motion

Dictate to your secretary while walking back and forth. This breaks up long periods of sitting, giving you light physical conditioning—and often has a dynamic impact on your sentence formulation.

Whenever possible, hold some talks—such as in negotiation breaks—during a walk. The vigor of the motion can carry over to your arguments and ideas.

Keep-Fit Tip No. 5: Every Joint Once

Make use of everyday opportunities to move every joint through its full scope at least once. Stretch as high as you can, bend over, do a deep knee bend, twist your torso, and rotate your shoulders.

After every long period of sitting (office, conference, flight, drive, television), really stretch your limbs.

Keep-Fit Tip No. 6: Tennis Ball Power

Keep an old tennis ball with you.

Now and then squeeze the ball firmly with each hand, using about two-thirds of your strength. Make sure that upper arm, chest, and shoulder muscles are also flexed.

Count to seven during muscle tightening, then relax.

Keep-Fit Tip No. 7: Stomach Press

Clasp your hands together, placing the palms against the slightly pulled-in abdomen.

Tense up the stomach muscles, using about two-thirds of your strength.

Press your hands firmly against the tightened stomach muscles. Count to seven, then relax.

Keep-Fit Tip No. 8: Towel Expander

Roll up a towel the long way and hold on to the ends. Sit on the floor with knees drawn up, towel in front of your feet.

Stretch feet against towel, simultaneously tensing arms and legs with two-thirds of your strength.

Count to seven, then relax.

Keep-Fit Tip No. 9: Shake Hands

Grasp the left hand with the right, as if you wanted to shake hands with yourself.

Squeeze with both hands, using two-thirds of your strength.
Count to seven, then relax.

Keep-Fit Tip No. 10: Moving Walls

Stand one pace away from a wall; place hands against wall at
shoulder height.
Press forcefully against wall, as if you could move it.
Count to seven, then relax.

This Lufthansa regimen won't turn you into Mr. or Miss Universe. But it may keep you from becoming Mr. or Miss Miserable.

13

How to Relax on the Plane

The physical fatigue you experience on any long flight tends to slow your reaction time and decrease your muscle tone. In addition, it triggers certain chemical changes in your body, increasing the lactic acid in your blood, reducing your blood glucose and (from perspiring in the desertlike cabin conditions) electrolytes. Sleeping (or at least relaxing) and exercising on board the plane help to fight this kind of fatigue. Fortunately, though, their benefits are not only physical but psychological, too.

During every mile you fly through the air, your progressive physical problems are being further compounded by the effects of mental fatigue. The longer you travel, the more mental fatigue accumulates. According to the aeromedical specialists, its symptoms are irritability, a shortened attention span, increased anxiety, and a tendency to be less cooperative.

In other words, those occasionally surly, inattentive, and uncooperative flight attendants you may encounter have a reason to be churlish. Mental fatigue in the air takes its toll, especially on pilots, who may be under their greatest tension at the very end of the trip. Flying has often been described as "hours and hours of boredom followed by a few seconds of stark terror."

Besides sleeping and exercising, is there anything else you can do aboard the aircraft to combat mental fatigue?

SOCIALIZING

"I hate flying—it's claustrophobic and a waste of time," insisted Andy Summer, drummer of the rock band The Police. Summer says he survives the band's worldwide, whirlwind schedule of international tours by sleeping—and then socializing. "I sleep a lot, and talk to other passengers if they're female," Summer said. "Otherwise," he added, "I just watch the stewardesses."

At least once, a social encounter Andy had on an airplane soon turned into a sexual one. Andy cherishes the day he became a full-fledged member of air travel's most exclusive club—the "mile-high club," limited to men or women who have figured out how to fornicate in midflight.

It isn't just rock stars whose sexual awareness peaks during an extended jet flight. Before I began to write about television, I wrote about sports. Early on, I was surprised to learn how many professional athletes, constantly shuttling from coast to coast, were married to former flight attendants. Now, scientists are providing proof that sexual interest does seem inclined to increase when time zones are crossed. No one is quite sure why. The heightened sexual awareness may result from the stimulus of encountering new people and places, or from stress, or simply from the peculiar configuration of an airplane seat, molding us into postures that activate our libidos. In any event, studies also show that sexual awareness suddenly diminishes again when the airplane lands and the acute phase of jet lag begins. Some scientists are convinced that this dip is connected to the depression so many passengers experience.

Whatever the cause of this curious airborne arousal, it is clearly helpful in combating jet lag. Anything that puts a passenger in a more social frame of mind is a definite plus. Aeromedical specialists have learned—not surprisingly, given man's gregarious nature—that social influences can affect jet lag; people traveling in package tours may be getting, along with their "free" shoulder bags, one more fringe benefit than they paid for. In jet lag tests conducted on soldiers flying between California and Asia, scientists discovered that military personnel traveling together in groups experienced less desynchronization when they landed than did loners. Tests of businessmen, too, indicate that they suffer fewer symptoms when they travel with companions.

"Obviously," commented one executive wryly, "it's only as an antidote to jet lag that so many of these guys have to take their secretaries along."

Whether your purpose is work or play, or a combination of both, traveling with a companion can soothe the jet lag syndrome. If you are traveling alone, however, that doesn't mean you have to lose out. Striking up a conversation with the person in the next seat can help—especially if that person not only is traveling alone, too, but belongs to the opposite sex. One salubrious side effect is that when you arrive, you may be able, on that first night, to engage in another activity recommended for reducing the impact of jet lag: sexual congress.

But you say you are too shy to strike up a conversation in an airplane with a complete stranger? If all else fails, here is one topic you can use to overcome your timidity. When you see him (or her) grimacing and clutching his head between his hands during takeoff, lean over and offer some sound advice to ease his suffering. Your "good Samaritan" routine may be rewarded: He won't think you're a pain in the neck if you can cure the pain in his ears.

CLOGGED EARS

Throughout, I've attributed certain distressful effects that occur in an airplane cabin—the one-third increase in potency of alcoholic beverages; the "synergistic" effect of alcohol mixing with medication; why soft drinks bloat your stomach—to the fact that, for technical reasons, modern jet aircraft are not completely pressurized. As your aircraft ascends, the atmospheric pressure surrounding it keeps falling. From about fifteen pounds per square inch at sea level, the pressure on your plane plummets to about four pounds per square inch at thirty-five thousand feet, your airplane's cruising level. That's about ten thousand feet above the altitude at which you could survive, on the outside, without an oxygen tank.

While you are climbing toward that cruising altitude, the air-conditioning system is sucking in air from the outside. So that you can breathe without putting on an oxygen mask, the air has to be compressed (in the jet engines) and heated; the air temperature outside your plane at cruising altitude is about minus-seventy degrees Fahrenheit. The outside air being drawn in isn't just extremely cold; it's extremely dry, too. That's why you have to keep drinking fruit juices or water throughout your flight. The only humidity in your airplane cabin comes from the moisture you and your fellow travelers provide by breathing and sweating.

However, because of the way your airplane is constructed and the dictates of the laws of physics that keep it flying, the air brought in from outside cannot be compressed to the altitude you are probably used to on the ground. Unless you reside in Denver, or Mexico City, or Quito, for example, your heart will have to work harder to supply your blood with its accustomed ratio of oxygen. Drinking a small Scotch, as we've seen, can leave you with a very large hangover. Smoking too many cigarettes can give you a temporary (and, of course, nonlethal) case of carbon-monoxide poisoning—and a terrific headache. And early on in aviation history, scientists learned that the decrease in atmospheric pressure that passengers experience aloft can give them a terrific earache, too.

In 1783 some intrepid doctors inaugurated the specialty of aeromedicine by launching into space, in a basket attached to a large balloon, a duck, a sheep, and a chicken. After floating around the sky for a while, the ark of astronauts descended to earth. The medical men were ecstatic to find that none of the animals had suffered symptoms of distress—none, at least, that the duck, the sheep, or the chicken cared to confide in them. Buoyed by their success, a few months later the aeromedical specialists sent up a man in the basket of the balloon. By the time the balloonist landed, however, he wasn't able to be any more revealing about his experience than his animal predecessors. He was too busy holding his ears and howling.

Why Your Ears Clog

The human ear, experts point out, is an extraordinary achievement of engineering. It is so sensitive that my seventeen-year-old son can hear the announcement of a seventeen-dollar-per-ticket rock concert on the radio while standing two blocks away, yet so flexible that when I stand right next to him and shout at him to straighten up his room, he acts absolutely deaf. The human ear, it seems, is a marvelous instrument for hearing things you want it to and not hearing things you don't. However, the human ear is not well designed to deal with the changes in air pressure that occur when jet planes gain or lose altitude.

The problem-prone part (at least in a jet cabin, at cruising altitude) is a tiny air sac called the middle ear. There would be no pressurization problem if the middle ear opened onto the ear canal, and thus to the outside. The problem then would be that you would probably be deaf. Instead of connecting to the ear canal, however, this air sac leads through the Eustachian tube to the rear of the nose, at the very spot where mucus coagulates. If the nose contains a lot of mucus and you are flying, the troubles begin.

In order to compress the outside air to an equivalent inside the plane of five thousand to seven thousand feet or more above sea level, what the jet's system is really doing is expanding the air in the middle ear, too—about 20 percent.

As the plane takes off or descends, the air pressure changes rapidly. If the Eustachian tube is unclogged, the air in the inner ear equalizes with the air pressure outside it. But if mucus bars the way, that expanded air in the inner ear gets trapped. The pressure of it trying to get out is what causes the pain you feel.

Remember, I suggested that you include in your medical kit a nasal spray or pill. If you use the decongestant a half-hour before you take off (just as your flight begins to board, for instance) and a half-hour before you land (when your pilot announces that he is going to begin his descent), it will shrink the swollen membranes in your nose and dissolve the mucus. However, for some people—pregnant women, people with a heart ailment or a thyroid condition, etc.—decongestants pose a medical risk. For them, and for anyone else who either forgets to bring along a nasal spray or prefers not to use one, Dr. Karl Neumann, medical adviser to *Travel & Holiday* magazine, offers some other suggestions.

Swallowing

At the airport, before you depart, stop by the candy counter and purchase a pack of mints. (You'll have time; remember, you are going to arrive at the airport early.) Just before you take off and also, later, before you begin the descent, pop a mint into your mouth and just let it melt. While the mint is melting, you are almost continuously swallowing. Swallowing keeps the Eustachian tubes open.

Of course, you don't really need mints to make you swallow. Normally, without realizing it, you swallow twice a minute, even if there's nothing but saliva in your mouth. However, when you are asleep, you swallow only half as often. So, especially on the descent, when you are liable still to be sleeping, make sure someone—a flight attendant or a friend—wakes you up.

Yawning

Yawning is an even more effective way to clear that clogged middle ear than swallowing. If that doesn't do the job, try swallowing or yawning with your nostrils pinched shut.

However, sometimes—especially if you have a cold or are suffering from some allergy—neither swallowing nor yawning will work. Dr. Neumann offers the following method for the time when all else fails:

Doomsday Ear Unclogger

The ultimate method to end the pain of clogged ears is

1. Pinch your nostrils shut.
2. Take a mouthful of air.
3. With your cheek and neck muscles, force the air into the back of your nose, says Dr. Neumann, "as if you were trying to blow your thumb and fingers off your nostrils." The moment you hear a loud pop in your ears, you'll know that you have won the battle against bottled-up air. If you get clogged up again, simply repeat steps one through three.

"When inflating your ears," Dr. Neumann added, "you should not use force from your chest (lungs) or abdomen (diaphragm), which can create pressures that are too high. The proper technique involves only pressure created by your cheek and throat muscles."

Now that you have overwhelmed the gal or gent in the seat next to you with your worldliness, helping her or him to clear those clogged ears, clear your own mind of everything but the simple comforts of companionship. Don't do any of the paperwork you brought along with you. Don't watch the movie. Just lie back and relax. Soon you will be landing at your destination. Eat breakfast; that sends a signal to your biological clock, telling it a new day has started. Raise the shade of the nearest window and look out at the sun; that sends another strong signal to your brain. If you followed the advice in this book, you can look forward to having a lot of fun. If not . . . jet lag will be waiting at the airport to greet you.

III
At Your Destination

14

When You Land

Several years ago, the newly appointed president of a major oil company's Far Eastern subsidiary relocated his family from Connecticut to Hong Kong, then blasted off on seven transpacific air flights in two weeks. "I became irritable," the executive recalled. "My eyes itched; I couldn't read much."

The executive's eighth trip was a transatlantic one, to corporate headquarters in New York. Executives from the parent company greeted him at the airport. They escorted him to a company helicopter, waiting to whisk him away to a meeting in Manhattan. "I thought one of those guys was trying to squeeze ahead of me getting into the helicopter," said the executive. "I dropped him right on his ass."

Later, in Hong Kong, the executive asked a company doctor to explain the bizarre behavior. The doctor listened to the executive's litany of symptoms. The remedy he prescribed was a local soup. "It's tasty," said the executive, "and it really does calm me down."

Now, after a trip back to the Orient across several time zones, the executive always samples a few bowls of that soothing broth—flavored with slices of python and cobra. Snake soup is an Asian antidote to jet lag.

However, if you've ignored my counsel up to now (and thus the advice of the aeromedical specialists and the scientists and the jet-setters), even snake soup won't do you any good; snake soup is no remedy for being snake-bit. If, on the other hand, you've practiced what I've been preaching, you'll reach your destination in fine shape to take on The Malady Itself—the disorientation of all your internal systems, and the symptoms that dislocation generates.

Your digestive system may be out of whack a day for each time zone you've crossed. Your heart rate may take five-and-a-half days to get back in sync, your body temperature eight days, your urine output ten days. The day following a long flight often becomes an out-of-focus print: ghostly, vague, smudged by jet lag's symptomatic fingerprints.

Which effects of jet lag are liable to cause you the most distress? What strategies can you devise to cope with them? The first difficulty you are likely to encounter involves sleep—the lack of it.

SLEEPING

Remember: Jet travel is easier on the system going west than east. Recently, a pair of scientists, Karl E. Klein and Hans Wegmann, conducted a study showing that during the first thirty to forty hours after a westbound flight, biological rhythms shifted between 20 to 80 percent more in phase than after an eastbound flight. Their experiments proved that even if your home is in the east, you tend to adapt more quickly after a westward flight.

This rule applies to sleeping patterns, too. Most people find it comparatively easy to adjust to the extended day flying westbound, say, from New York to Los Angeles. All you have to do is force yourself to keep awake an extra three hours, and you can go to sleep when the natives do. You may awaken three hours earlier than they do for the first few days, but that's an inconvenience you can turn to advantage by accomplishing more work or more touring in those additional daylight hours. However, as I pointed out before, if you are an early riser, a westbound flight can still present some problems.

"It was harder for me going west than it was coming east," said a female television executive who frequently commutes between coasts. "Staying up the extra three hours, I found that first night's sleep very difficult. My body twitched. The next day, at around five or six o'clock in the evening, I got very tired. It took about two days," she added, "before I could get past five or six without feeling the need to go to sleep."

The executive says that she deals with her sleeplessness by taking, on her first night on the West Coast, about two-and-a-half milligrams of Valium before she goes to bed. In contrast, eastbound travelers are unlikely to find a drug potent enough to put them into dreamland.

Eastbound

If you traveled to Europe from the United States, although a morning departure would have been better, you most probably departed when most passengers do, in the dead of night. Now you have arrived. You are at your hotel, feeling so fatigued that you are convinced that if you flopped on your bed you wouldn't awaken until tomorrow morning. But should you sleep? Should you stay awake? Which tactic will quicken the adjustment of your internal day-night cycle so that it matches the normal rhythm of the natives?

"The thing that really can screw you up—it used to really screw me up years ago when I first started going over to Europe—is you stay up on the flight because you're not tired, and then you get there, go to bed, and you sleep the whole first day," said Don Ohlmeyer, NBC's ex-head of sports and now an independent packager and producer of programming. "You're dead. Case closed. You might as well go home." Ohlmeyer added, "You are now into the syndrome where you are tired all day and awake all night. I've always found that you are better off shocking your system into submission, rather than trying to gradually ease into a new cycle."

Many scientists agree. Although the temptation to sleep off your jet lag may be almost irresistible, Dr. Elliot Weitzman, expert in sleep research at the Laboratory of Human Chronophysiology at Montefiore Hospital in New York, warns the newly arrived to resist. "Reasonable evidence indicates that we can will awakeness, whereas we cannot make ourselves fall asleep," said Dr. Weitzman. "Maintaining wakefulness should force the adjustment to be made more quickly." Even if your lack of sleep results in mental fogginess or loss of short-term memory, Dr. Weitzman argues that the benefits, for coping with jet lag, outweigh these inconveniences. "It is important to remain active during the daytime in order to successfully make the phase shift," he insisted.

The best method of making sure you don't succumb to sleep (if it's 8 A.M. in Paris, it's 2 A.M. back home in New York) is to spend as much as possible of that first day abroad away from your hotel room. Take a short stroll around the city; if the weather permits, lunch at a sidewalk café. Pass the afternoon in a park; almost every major world capital has at least one, and a park bench is a marvelous window. You can sit there and recover from culture shock—watching the people, absorbing the music of their language—in easy, effortless stages. And you'll be helping yourself to recover from jet lag, too.

Travelers who do remain relatively isolated, the scientists say, seem to take longer to adjust than ones who tour in groups or simply spend some time outdoors. Hidden in your hotel room, you can't begin to sop up social and temporal cues. At your destination as well as in the airplane, it seems, social stimuli play a crucial role in regulating your biological rhythms.

That night, you eat dinner when the natives do, then go to sleep. It's that easy.

The problem is *staying* asleep.

"You get over there and you're exhausted, and the first night you wake up at 2 A.M., at 3:30 A.M., and at 5 A.M.," said ABC's Jim McKay, whose more than a quarter of a million air miles each year rank high among America's jet-setters. "You think: 'My God, what am I going to do?' "

Unless you managed to completely preadapt your pattern before you departed, on that first night abroad your sleep rhythms may undergo some distressing changes. Researchers investigating the effects of time-zone passage on sleep have discovered that REM (rapid eye movement) sleep (when you experience the deep dreaming deemed essential for mental health) was both delayed and truncated. In fact, although test subjects' natural rhythms showed signs of reasserting themselves beginning with the second night abroad, the volunteers slept fitfully, and woke up earlier than usual, for as many as five days.

The majority of subjects who participated in the experiments were in their twenties. Like seventeen-year-old tennis star Andrea Jaeger, they had less trouble twisting their conventional sleep patterns into new ones. "I just go to sleep and don't worry about what time it is in Chicago," said Jaeger.

The few tested who were in their forties suffered particularly severe REM disruption and were prone to awaken early even longer. Some travelers' sleep rhythms may take as many as fourteen days to return to normal.

What do you do when you wake up at three in the morning, without even being able to take a dose of late-night television as a sedative? (Most television abroad is government controlled and thus indescribably dull; mercifully, it usually shuts down around midnight.) Each jet-setter seems to have evolved his own prescription. Morley Safer may get out of bed, turn on the light, and dash off a quick roomscape. "I find painting marvelously therapeutic," said Safer. "I won't fly without some sort of paint box and brushes."

Jim McKay, on the other hand, makes sure he brings along some entertaining reading material for just such an emergency. McKay says that using reading to rout sleeplessness is an honored family tradition. "Before jet lag, my father-in-law always had a sleeplessness problem," McKay recalled. "And one of the famous family stories was, he woke up in the middle of the night and there wasn't even a Gideon Bible in the room. He finally opened all the drawers of the bureau. One of them happened to be lined with a newspaper ten years old. So," McKay added, "he read it."

It is important, however, not to stay up too long. Don't get carried away, or else you'll never get your sleep pattern in sync with those of the natives. Sleep deprivation can become an increasingly troublesome burden to the traveler, especially if he has to constantly shift through time zones without ever having enough time to adjust to any particular one. Air France allows its pilots credit for extra flight time on long east-west or west-east routes. British Airways learned that its crews could only cope with a mounting sleep deficit for a maximum of eight days.

EXERCISING

One way to help sleep to come that first night is to make sure you do some exercising that first day (and each day that follows, too). More Americans are more active than ever before, and physical involvement in some kind of sport is an essential part of their daily routine. If you are not a part-time jock, don't suddenly jump into the hotel pool and start paddling till you get seasick. On the other hand, if you are a tennis player, some light activity between the lines may help your body relax enough to induce sleep.

"For a number of years, I was kind of reluctant to go to Europe, except for the biggest tournaments," said Billie Jean King, who still ranks among the top women tennis pros at the "ancient" age of thirty-nine. "In too many places, there just weren't any facilities I could use to stay in shape. Now," she added, "almost everywhere you go, Europe or Asia, plenty of health clubs have sprung up. For a small fee, if you're a visitor, many of them will let you use their facilities on a short-term basis."

Your own hotel may have a pool or a whirlpool. You can use either one to help wash away the tension that keeps you tossing and turning at night. Joggers may want to wait a day before pursuing so strenuous an activity. If you are a dedicated and accomplished runner, however, a short prance through the local park may do you more good than harm. In your hotel room, as well, you can perform brief sets of exercises that help you relax, and thus aid in readjusting your internal cycles. I quoted Lufthansa's first ten "Keep-Fit Tips" on pages 99–101. If you get tired of doing those simple exercises in your hotel room (or during business conferences), ask the concierge at your hotel for the address of the nearest toy store. Go and purchase a jump rope. Jumping rope for a quarter of an hour, say the kinesiologists, is the equivalent of running a mile.

Of course, if you are lucky enough to be traveling with a companion of the opposite sex (or have become on intimate terms with one along the way), there is one more "exercise" you can practice which scientists recommend as an aid to sleep and thus as an armament in the war against jet lag. According to the researchers' observations, sexual activity can relieve travelers' insomnia by relaxing the body enough to induce sleep. After reaching its apex sometime during your flight, your libido will plummet to its nadir soon after you land. By the time night falls, however, you may have recovered just enough to surrender to that attractive companion's charms.

15

Peaks and Troughs

For the casual tourist, jet lag can be a nuisance. Forewarned, however, he can adapt his schedule to minimize the major risks. Knowing that a long flight through too many time zones seriously impairs manual dexterity, for instance, he can arrange to postpone renting a car abroad for a day or two, instead of traveling by taxi or bus or train. Businessmen and professionals, in contrast, often can't afford the luxury of waiting for time itself to mend their inner clocks. They may have to perform at their peak under appalling mental and physical conditions.

"The more time zones you cross, the crosser people tend to become," said "60 Minutes" correspondent Harry Reasoner. "Co-workers get short tempers over things they'd normally shrug off."

"Mood *is* affected," confirmed Dr. David Moreau, who, in Project Pegasus, studied the effects of jet lag on volunteers shuttling between England and California. "It was no accident that nearly all the six female volunteers burst into spontaneous tears the night they got back from California."

Men may feel compelled to cover up their feelings, but they also suffer from the same emotional distress. Memory gets muddled, too. Scientists say that severe jet lag can engender a temporary amnesia; mice trained over a long period of time to find food at the end of a maze suddenly "forgot how" when their laboratory day-night cycle was altered. Other symptoms can disrupt a business traveler's routine even more seriously.

One winter day in 1964, ABC's Jim McKay was bundled up against a chill Austrian morning, standing before a backdrop of snow-covered mountains near Innsbruck. He was about to ad-lib, for the videotape cameras, a three-minute introduction that would set the scene for the upcoming Winter Olympics. "We'd been traveling for months. We'd arrived the night before," McKay recalled, "driving through a snowstorm to get to the hotel, and ending up with two or three hours of sleep. Normally, I can knock off a three-minute ad-lib the first time around. That morning," he added, "near Innsbruck, it took me *twenty-two takes.*"

Of course, television personalities aren't the only professionals whose performance may be adversely affected by crossing time zones. For example, Brinks' couriers, escorting around-the-world shipments of cash, securities, or gold bullion are vulnerable, too. Insurance laws stipulate that they have to stand guard beside the airplane's cargo hatch while the plane is on the ground, so even while the aircraft is refueling, they cannot rest. Airline pilots are also prone.

"It's not the flying that's so difficult," a pilot with thirty-five years experience told Mike Wallace on "60 Minutes." "We discipline ourselves so much we could fly in a fatigued situation. It's the mental decisions," he added. "It's the possibility of wanting to get into an airport so badly that you allow yourself to make a decision that you really shouldn't make."

Businessmen and professionals who need to be sharp during the first few days after they arrive may have to adopt a set of specific strategies.

DECISION MAKING

Before you departed, you should have made sure, if possible, not to schedule any crucial conferences during your first day abroad. Once you arrive, you should avoid making any major decisions for a few days, too. Tests show that soundness of judgment may be 20 percent less than your best performance. It may take anywhere from five or six days, if you traveled westbound, and up to nine days, if you journeyed to the east, before your grasp of numerical problems and other mental gymnastics returns to normal.

Lester W. Pullen, president (Asia-Pacific) of R. J. Reynolds Tobacco Company, agrees that executives are silly to make crucial decisions soon after deplaning from long flights. "But," he added, "you tell me, how can the president of a company step off a plane and take a twenty-four-hour rest? The most powerful incentive is to go straight into a meeting and show everybody how tough you are."

How can an executive abroad keep from becoming a victim of the new time cycle? By trying some tactics designed to turn time into an ally.

KEEPING ON HOME TIME

"I commend the Russians' concept of keeping all airport clocks throughout their eleven time zones on Moscow time," said author James Michener, who has spent many hours soaring over the icy tundra. "The jet lag," Michener added, "seems less that way."

When Harold Geneen was chairman of ITT, he and other ITT corporate executives jetting to Europe conducted meetings on New York time the first day, at the urging of ITT's medical staff. Robert Barry, as supervisor of special services for Brinks, used to fly off to Hong Kong, Tokyo, or Rio nearly every week; he always wore a watch on each wrist. He ate and slept by the one set to New York time, and kept the other set to local time, for his appointments.

Aer Lingus also suggests that businessmen "try to retain sleeping and eating schedules on home time initially. This," the airline added in a brochure, "is analogous to orbiting astronauts who remain on Cape Kennedy time. The fortunate East Coast businessman who could keep on home time would get up at 6 A.M. New York time, let us say, even if the locals considered it midday, and had lunch on their minds instead of breakfast. He would have the local afternoon to communicate with his European clients and associates. The executive can adapt to local time gradually," concluded the Aer Lingus pamphlet, "by adjusting his regimen by about an hour each day."

However, some business travelers regard this tactic with skepticism, suggesting it has in-built disadvantages that may outweigh its assets. Harry Reasoner remembers that when President Lyndon Johnson met Vietnam's president Nguyen Van Thieu on Guam in 1967, he kept himself on Oval Office time during the entire sixty-seven-hour trip.

"That wouldn't work for people in this business," said Reasoner. "I mean, none of us has the impact abroad of a president. The foreigners we deal with might be a little concerned for our mental health," he added, "if we started inviting them to lunch at ten o'clock at night."

In fact, keeping on home time is a tactic that probably can benefit the traveler flying west more than one flying east. Given the five- or six-hour time difference (depending on whether we are on daylight-saving time) between most of our East Coast cities and their European counterparts, keeping on your East Coast schedule can cause complications. Up until the early evening, local European time, you wouldn't face many problems. If you woke up at midday local time, you'd be ready for breakfast at about 1 P.M. and lunch at 7 P.M. The problems would begin when your stomach started telling you it was time for dinner, say at 7 P.M., home time. That would be 1 A.M. local time, an unlikely hour for native chefs to be nurturing a paella or a plate of pasta. Three hours later, you would go to bed—at 4 A.M. local time.

However, there is a way that eastbound travelers can turn this strange home timetable to peculiar advantage over the natives.

TURNING JET LAG TO YOUR ADVANTAGE

We are so-called day animals, which means that our ability to perform efficiently follows a definite progression through time. The highs and lows of every person's performance more or less keep, over any twenty-four-hour cycle, to a specific curve—substantiated by many experiments, and illustrated on the next page in a diagram by a German scientist named Wilhelm Graf. Notice that performance peaks about 8 A.M. and falls to its trough about 3 A.M.

What happens to this peak-and-trough pattern when you cross time zones? A 1970 study by Karl E. Klein and others revealed that, traveling from the United States to Europe, the old schedule persisted in the body for up to three days at the new destination, even while subjects were adapting to the new schedule. So for as long as this phenomenon lasted, the subjects of the experiment had *two peaks* and *two troughs* every day, one set on their American home time and one set on European time.

For instance, consider the performance curve of someone traveling on business from Europe to the United States. For the first few days, his pair of peaks would be roughly between 8 A.M. and 9 A.M. (the new schedule) and between 2 A.M. and 3 A.M., U.S.

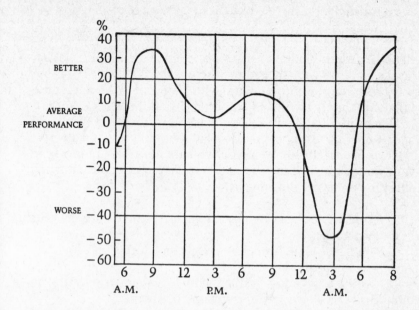

time (the old schedule). If he could find an American willing to transact business at 3 A.M., the European would have a distinct advantage. Unfortunately, of course, the only "business" that tends to be conducted at 3 A.M. in this country is . . . monkey business.

Traveling eastbound, however, the tactic can be exceedingly productive. You are going to be at your sharpest at 8 A.M. and 6 P.M., home time, which translate to 2 P.M. and midnight, European time. Looking at Graf's diagram above, you'll see that your pair of "up" periods coincide with your European counterpart's lethargic ones. If you schedule an important conference, say, between 2 P.M. and 3 P.M., European time (8 A.M. and 9 A.M., your home time), you should be about 30 percent sharper than he is. If you can arrange that conference for the evening, so much the better. By the time midnight European time rolls around, your business opponent will be struggling to keep his eyes open, while you will just be hitting your second peak of the day.

On the other hand, during your first few days in Europe you should reject any offer of an early-morning meeting. Nine o'clock in the morning finds your European friend at his peak, and you

at your daily performance trough. It's 3 A.M., according to your·
home body-time.

"The problem with these scientific studies and recommenda-
tions for people in our industry," complained Jim McKay, "is that
by the time we get adjusted to where we're going, we're on our
way back. I once went to Australia for a weekend," McKay added.
"I felt absolutely awful and I didn't recover for a week or more."

"That's nothing," said ABC producer-director Doug Wilson. "I
once went to Tokyo *for the day*—and I haven't recovered yet!"

Nevertheless, for those of you who are not likely to break up
your workweek with an "overnight" in Tibet, I offer the following
checklist on peaks and troughs:

1. Avoid scheduling any crucial business conference on your
first day abroad.

2. Don't make any important decisions during the first few
days at your destination.

3. If you are traveling westbound on a business trip lasting no
more than three days, try keeping on your home time.

4. If you are traveling eastbound on a business trip lasting no
longer than three days, not only keep on your home time but try
to make your foreign associates meet with you at your peak-
performance times.

And remember: If you are traveling to Europe on a night flight,
don't go to sleep when you arrive. Stay up, and sack out when
the natives do.

16

San Francisco-itis

Although it was more than twenty years ago, even now I can evoke the images that impressed me on my first trip to Europe. I can see the cathedral at Chartres, the Coliseum in Rome. I recall a dusty, steaming arena in Madrid, where the matador El Cordobes paraded in his spangled "suit of light," brandishing with one up-thrust hand the ears and tail of the brave bull he had dispatched, while his other hand caught flowers from the crowd.

I recall my astonishment upon leaving London's Heathrow Airport and realizing that nowadays Englishmen don't commute to work by bicycle. I remember how surprised I was to learn that America didn't invent the urban sprawl of multiple dwellings; the ancient Romans had their tenements, too. But most of all, etched vividly in my memory is the startling contrast between how regally the Europeans dined—and how wretchedly, to an American, they disposed of their personal biological wastes.

For weeks in Paris I walked around with a bursting bladder, refusing to submit my naked calves (it was summer and I was wearing shorts) to the bemused scrutiny of passers-by peering under a *pissoir*. I could accept, in the sleeping compartment of a French train, seeing in the semidark a beautiful young Frenchwoman enter and casually disrobe completely before climbing into the *couchette* opposite mine. I could even accept the parsimony of the tightwad concierge of a seedy hotel in Bordeaux, who, while I was reading one night in bed, opened my door a crack and reached in and switched off the light. But the state of continental bathrooms was culture shock I couldn't tolerate.

You enter the "rest room" of some elegant restaurant and find only a sink. No urinal, no toilet. Then you notice a sloping center section, with a hole in the middle, surrounded by a pair of massive

footprints. Is this some sort of shrine, you wonder—a Gallic equivalent to Hollywood's Grauman's Chinese Theater? Not quite.
Crouching over the hole, with your feet placed on the footprints,
you perform, and pull the dangling chain. Miraculously (since you
never see the source), a torrent of cleansing water fills the narrow
canyons carved beside, and below, your feet.

I lived in Europe for nearly six years. Only twice in that time
did I ever get trapped into using one of those "primitive" public
lavatories. Unfortunately, if you are not careful, you may wind
up spending far more time in that distressing (for a traveler used
to American hygienic amenities) mode.

A survey conducted among American students who had spent
a summer abroad revealed that about half had been smitten by
diarrhea. Students traveling in the hotter climates were afflicted
at an even higher rate. Over a quarter of the students who ventured
to Mexico, for example, were felled by the malady within the first
ten days. We Americans call the illness Montezuma's revenge.
The Mexicans, in turn, refer to it as San Francisco-itis. I once
journeyed to Mexico by car and passed two weeks eating only
native food and drinking the local water. I didn't get diarrhea till
the return trip home, when I ate some unripe apples from a road-
side stand in Virginia.

The fact is that whether you are traveling to the United States
or away from it, "traveler's diarrhea" is no laughing matter. It
can keep you from eating, from sleeping, from conducting business, and it interrupts your itinerary with dozens of unwanted
stops. If you aren't able to avoid contracting diarrhea or if you
can't cope with it once you do, "Crouching across a Continent"
may be the only appropriate title for your trip.

THE CAUSES

No one is quite sure why so many tourists get jet lag–compounding diarrhea when they travel, for the symptoms (nausea, head-
and stomach aches, even vomiting, accompanied by an inability
to retain matter in the intestines) can result from an array of
different causes. What *is* clear is that the disease is more common
among people traveling from a more temperate climate to one
that's more tropical and that it tends to strike younger persons
more often than older ones. Researchers suspect that the young

are more susceptible for reasons that have to do with their life-style rather than any biological predisposition. Younger travelers—often hitchhiking during the hot summer months—have less money to spend, which means they can't afford to be overly selective with regard to what they eat or drink. They may overindulge in food and drink. They may indiscriminately imbibe the local water and wine. These are the sparks that can ignite an intestinal explosion.

The "fuel" these activities ignite, causing the form of diarrhea that almost 90 percent of the time strikes a traveler abroad, are bacteria everyone in the entire world carries in his intestines. The only difference is that our own bacteria's cousins in warmer climates are a more virulent form. When we absorb them into our system, they tend to overpower their native American counterparts and cause all sorts of problems. To prevent being stricken by these malevolent creatures, you have to be careful of what you eat and what you drink.

FOOD

- Avoid eating any fruit that doesn't come your way intact, with the skin unpeeled. In other words, pass up that tempting sliced-fruit platter in a restaurant.
- Order your vegetables well cooked. In some Third World countries, farmers still use human waste instead of chemical fertilizers. Unfriendly bacteria can be transmitted from a native to you via contact with human waste.
- Avoid raw oysters unless your restaurateur can provide a pedigree, proving his oysters weren't gathered in polluted waters.
- Don't drink milk (or milk products) unless you see the milk being boiled. Pasteurization hasn't caught on yet in many countries, including some rural outposts of the good doctor's native France.
- Make sure your meats come well cooked. Ask for a "rare" steak, and you may end up with a not-so-rare case of diarrhea, or some internal parasite.

But use common sense. A well-recommended restaurant (recommended, say, by Michelin, Fielding, or another respected travel

guide) will undoubtedly have taken precautions to prevent sending its diners home with the trots. Where you really have to watch
out is in Europe's and Asia's backwaters, and in many areas of
Africa and South America.

DRINK

- If you are not a confirmed wine drinker, go easy on the *vin
  locale*. If you do need wine with your meal, avoid the practice
  Americans are used to. Suckers for salesmanship, we are
  taught by Madison Avenue to ask for wines by their brand
  names. In Europe—where, despite those wine tasters you see
  on American TV, the good wines are far superior to anything
  California can produce—wines are known only by the region
  the grape comes from and by the year of the harvest. If some
  shop owner offers you a brand-name wine in continental
  Europe (the English know even less about wines than we do),
  simply say no. It's probably some rotgut the locals refuse to
  drink.
     The safest tactic is to purchase some relatively expensive
  bottled regional wine. But if you really wanted to play it safe,
  you would have stayed home.
     Whenever I travel, particularly in countries proud of their
  wines (such as France, Germany, Spain, Chile, etc.), I try to
  determine the wine of the local region, and I drink that. Enter
  a bar and ask a native. It won't take much Spanish, for instance, in that country's northern Basque provinces, to as-
  certain that the locals prefer red over white, and stick to
  grapes grown in the region of Rioja. They'll drink theirs right
  out of the barrel, in tiny glasses. You do what they do. They
  know wines—the good ones and the bad ones. That barreled
  wine will be the best and the safest and the cheapest.
     My mother-in-law, a Spanish Basque, used to spend her
  summers in a house near a factory where a brand of sangria,
  famous in America but unknown in Spain, was made. She
  swears that although wine kept coming out by the caseload,
  no grapes ever entered. Not long ago, an Italian company was
  fined for filling bottles exported abroad with "wine" watered
  down with horse urine. Stick to the barrels instead of the
  cheap, brand-name, bottled stuff.

- The directions regarding the local water supply are just the opposite. In many communities around the world, once-pure water supplies have become contaminated with dangerous bacteria. Don't worry about being called a cultural philistine—*Don't drink the water!* The Europeans don't. They drink wine or beer (foreign brands are extraordinarily good, not only in the Nordic countries but in lower-latitude nations like Spain and Mexico, too). Furthermore, everywhere there are safe, salubrious brands of bottled water (carbonated and uncarbonated), far cheaper than the chic French one people prefer in expense-account New York restaurants. Brand-name carbonated soda waters will do, as well.
- Avoid the overuse of iced drinks. The last thing your body—plagued by jet lag—needs is too many ice-cold internal showers.

THE CURE

What do you do if, despite your best-laid plans, the malady strikes anyway? To begin with, stop eating solid foods and start drinking plenty of fluids. Beyond that, you can find a dizzying array of antidiarrhea drugs at your nearest pharmacy. (In many foreign countries, pharmacists have far more authority to dispense medications than do their U.S. peers.) Don't necessarily ask for the medicine you usually use at home, Kaopectate, since this medication probably won't help cure that particular brand of "traveler's diarrhea" you've contracted. Let the pharmacist recommend something he has faith in.

But be careful, especially you women, that he understands your problem. A couple of years ago, in Spain, my wife and I both suffered terrible cases of San Francisco-itis, after staying overnight in a sixteenth-century castle that had no air conditioning. The next morning, still wretched, we drove to the town square and parked in front of a pharmacy. As my wife, a Spaniard, got out of the car to enter the store, she vomited. The pharmacist saw that and saw her holding her stomach. Putting one and one together—her symptoms and the early hour—the pharmacist and some women customers immediately ran out and solicitously ushered my wife into the store. Only the fact that she spoke Spanish saved her from being sold pills to soothe the effects of pregnancy morning sickness.

Of course, if you can avoid taking medication, so much the better. In fact, the U.S. Public Health Service offers a pamphlet containing a nonmedicinal method you might want to try. The remedy is designed to put back in your body the glucose and potassium you've lost, while restoring the balance of salts in your system depleted by dehydration. The formula is:

Put two normal-size drinking glasses on the table in front of you.

In glass number one put:

> 8 ounces of any fruit juice
> ½ teaspoon of honey or corn syrup
> 1 pinch of ordinary table salt

In glass number two, put:

> 8 ounces of carbonated water or water that has been thoroughly boiled
> ¼ teaspoon of baking soda

Thoroughly mix the contents of each glass. Then pick up one glass in each hand. Sip first from one, then the other, then the first one again—and so on, until you've drained both glasses. Follow up with some more carbonated soda water or Seltzer water, or drink some hot tea. If the remedy works, thank your Uncle Sam's wife Samantha.

But what if this cure for Montezuma's revenge doesn't work? What can you do if you are at your destination, and *nothing* works, because you ignored the advice and counsel of the scientists and the jet-setters? No sermon I can offer will cure your suffering. So, instead, I'll offer you a song. Doug Wilson, the globe-hopping ABC Sports producer/director/composer wrote it.

"I've had a joyous time, a number of times, singing this for my fellow-passengers at forty thousand feet," Doug recalled. "Once when I sang this on an airplane," he added, "a flight attendant invited me to a meeting of an organization called Clipped Wings, so that I could serenade some nostalgic ex-stewardesses."

Doug never boards a plane without his guitar. If you happen to be traveling on that aircraft, too, you'll hear him begin to moan this plaintive dirge as the plane starts descending into your new time zone. He calls it "My Home Time Zone Blues" or sometimes "Jet Lag Blues." ("It depends at forty thousand feet," Doug says, "whether I can remember it or not.")

When I fly, across the sky,
To places far beyond me.
My body slips through time zones,
And confusion sits upon me.
I set my feet down upon the ground
In a place I wasn't born in.
And then I stand and I look around,
And it's twilight in the mornin'.

(Chorus)
Take me back to my home time zone, oh yeah,
My home time zone.
I'm always a mess when I get to my address
In my home time zone.

Oh, all the doctors and professors
Can't seem to learn just what it is
That happens to a man
When he flies across the land
A-thinkin' he's a jet set whiz.
Some people call it jet lag,
And other people say they're just distressed.
I only know that when I get home
I am just a mess.

(Chorus)
Take me back to my home time zone—etc.

When all the world becomes confusion
Everythin' you see is just illusion
You're lookin' desperately
For your memory,
And all you've got left is delusion.
Your body's come apart, there's palpitation in your heart,

And your brain's in a terrible state.
You think you're altogether, but you might as well surrender.
'Cause, man, you are now a flake.

    (Chorus)
Get back to your home time zone—etc.

Now, in this modern day and age,
When travelin' is all of the current rage,
You'd think they'd have found the key
To this modern malady.
Well, I can explain
What happens in a plane.
Nature is corrupt.
It ain't scientific, but my answer is specific.
You're just plain all messed up.

    (Chorus)
Back to your home time zone, oh yeah,
Your home time zone.
You're always a mess when you get to your address
In your home time zone. . . .
Stewardess—would you mind bringing Rolaids with
my Beaujolais!

Index

Index